THE BREAD WHICH WE BREAK

THE BREAD WHICH WE BREAK

G. D. YARNOLD

Warden of
St. Deiniol's Library, Hawarden

LONDON
OXFORD UNIVERSITY PRESS
NEW YORK TORONTO
1960

Oxford University Press, Amen House, London E.C.4

GLASGOW NEW YORK TORONTO MELBOURNE WELLINGTON
BOMBAY CALCUTTA MADRAS KARACHI KUALA LUMPUR
CAPE TOWN IBADAN NAIROBI ACCRA

Printed in Great Britain by
Northumberland Press Limited
Gateshead on Tyne

PREFACE

This book is about the Eucharist. It is written by an Anglican, but not addressed to Anglicans only. It is untechnical, but not untheological; wide in its sympathies (at least in intention), but I hope neither nebulous nor unorthodox. The title itself, drawn from St. Paul, demands that we think in a particular way about the Eucharist—and St. Paul is very much up-to-date in this matter. 'The Bread' is the eucharistic loaf, but also ourselves in Christ. 'We' is all Christian people, not simply those of one closed ecclesiastical system. 'Break' is what we are commanded by Christ to do when we celebrate the sacrament of the Church's unity: and also (in another sense) what we do when we fail to realize the unity which Christ has given.

'The Bread which we Break' is intended therefore to draw Christians together, through a deeper understanding of what we already have in common in our eucharistic worship, even in a divided Christendom; and I can only hope that what is written in charity will be so judged.

G.D.Y.

St. Deiniol's Library,
  Hawarden.
    October 1959.

Contents

Do This in Remembrance of Me

For the benefit of his contemporaries in the mid-second century, Justin Martyr wrote a well-known and much-quoted account of the Christian Eucharist. To-day such a task would be more difficult, on account of the increased diversity of Christian practice; and also somewhat super-fluous, because of the complete disappearance of the secrecy which once surrounded the worship of the Church. Indeed it can be taken for granted that almost any reader of this book is already familiar with the Chris-tian Eucharist by one or other of its names, and accord-ing to the tradition of that branch of the Christian Church in which he has been nourished. For him this *is* the Eucharist. He is aware, of course, of the diversity of traditions, as he is aware of their common origin in the Supper of the Lord. What he seeks to understand is the manner in which the Eucharist, as he knows it, has descended from the prototype instituted by the Lord himself; what is the relationship between the divergent traditions of to-day; and what is the underlying theo-logical meaning of the rite itself.

Now it is altogether apparent that no particular Eucharist exists in isolation, or stands by itself. Each celebration is one of a series of essentially similar acts: a series which reaches out in more than one direction.

Each Eucharist is linked (in space) with every other altar on earth; in the next parish, in the next diocese, in distant lands, across denominational barriers of man's devising. It is linked in time; backwards, through the Church of previous ages to the Eucharist of the Apostles themselves, and to the Lord's Supper; forward in time till he comes. It is linked in eternity to the 'heavenly altar' at which our great High Priest offers his own perfect sacrifice eternally. And this community of eucharistic action is simply the consequence of the fact that in all ages and in all places the Church does what her Lord commanded her to do, when he took bread and broke it, saying, 'Do this in remembrance of me.' The same, and essential, and unchanging act of Christian worship is offered Sunday by Sunday, and day by day, wherever and whenever the Church obeys her Lord's command. Thus, in space, in time, and in eternity, every particular Eucharist is linked with every other, past, present and future.

When we ask, however, which is the prior link, we may be tempted to answer: the link in time, by which each eucharistic action is descended in a time-sequence from the Lord's Supper itself, and by which continuity of tradition is maintained. But this would be to mistake successiveness for true continuity: to ignore the interval of twenty-four hours (or more) which separates each Eucharist from the previous celebration at the same altar. The fact is that whenever or wherever the eucharistic action is performed, eternity impinges upon time: the Church on earth is caught up into the Church in heaven. 'Therefore with Angels and Archangels, and with all the company of heaven, we laud and magnify thy glorious Name; evermore praising thee, and saying, Holy, holy,

holy . . .' It is this contact with eternity, this link with the timeless, which is primary. Both logically and theologically, each separate eucharistic action upon earth is linked first of all with Christ's own perfect offering, eternal in the heavenly places; and thence backwards and forwards in time, and outwards in space. The eucharistic action of the Church on earth is one, precisely because it is one with the eternal worship of heaven itself.

Moreover, what is done in each Eucharist which the Church celebrates on earth derives its meaning from the eternal fact of Christ's perfect self-offering. In the time-sequence of human history the New Testament picks out three separate events, each of which expresses one aspect of Christ's self-offering. Not all are events in precisely the same sense. Indeed, in all but the first the normal sense of the word ' event' is transcended. First, the Passion of our Lord is the faithful acceptance of suffering and death, by which his unique and perfect life is laid down on man's behalf. Second, the Resurrection is the vindication of that perfect life by the Father; and the appearances are the declaration to mankind of that vindication. Third, the Ascension is the inevitable exaltation of the Incarnate Son to the Throne of heaven, which declares his true status, and lifts human nature into the heavenly places. The three events taken together express the bringing of the perfect sacrifice into the eternal sanctuary. And the doctrine of the eternal self-offering of Christ at the heavenly altar, worked out in detail in the Epistle to the Hebrews, is in its turn the completion of the Passion–Resurrection–Ascension series of events. In the Passion, time was linked with eternity; eternity had burst into time, and taken possession of it. In the Ascension, time was transcended, lifted up into eternity. Henceforward we know Christ no more 'after the flesh' (2 Cor. 5.16); that is to say, under the conditions imposed by space and time; but in knowing him we ourselves are lifted up, transiently, into the eternal world. In our experience of the Ascended Christ we move, as it were, in a new dimension. The Eucharist is the most intimate of the ways in which we know Christ after this manner.

In the Supper, immediately before the Passion–Resurrection–Ascension series of events was set in motion, the Lord performed that symbolic act which declared the significance of those events; commanding the disciples to repeat what he did. The breaking of the bread and the blessing of the cup express symbolically the eternal fact of Christ's perfect self-offering; just as surely as the Passion–Resurrection–Ascension series of events expresses the same eternal fact on the plane of history and beyond history. The Eucharist derives its meaning from Christ's self-offering. Every time the eucharistic action is performed in obedience to the command, 'Do this in remembrance of me', the eternal fact of Christ's perfect self-offering is both recalled and declared. By this simple act of obedience, constantly repeated, the eucharistic worship of the Church is created and sustained through time and space. Each Eucharist is linked to the eternal offering of Christ in the heavenly places. At each celebration, time is transcended, and the eternal bursts through again into the temporal. The worshipping congregation is lifted up to share in the worship of heaven; and to identify itself afresh with the perfect offering of the 'Lamb slain from the foundation of the world' (Rev. 13.8) who 'shall reign for ever and ever' (Rev. 11.15).

What the Church believes about the Eucharist can be expressed in a great variety of ways. No one system of eucharistic theology can possibly exhaust the whole truth, for the mystery indeed passes human understanding. One person may prefer to express the mystery in one way, another in another; but different human expressions of a single deep truth tend to be complementary rather than conflicting. It is more important to affirm what one knows oneself out of Christian experience, than to deny another's affirmation. To their shame Christian people have sometimes wrangled uncharitably over differing interpretations of the Eucharist: a fact which means, at the very least, that it is impossible to overestimate the importance of what is believed about the Eucharist. But the fact that the Church *does* what Christ commanded it to do is of even greater importance. Some branches of the Church are accustomed to celebrate the Eucharist in a liturgy which expresses the historic belief of Christendom with great fulness, and with an elaborate ceremonial which adds both dignity and persuasiveness to the rite. Others are accustomed to a relative bareness both of expression and of outward observance. What is of supreme significance, however, is that almost without exception organized Christianity has been obedient to the command, '*Do* this in remembrance of me.'

By the simple fact of obedience, and by no other means, eucharistic worship exists, is sustained, and is ever repeated. The blessings and benefits of the sacrament are therefore available to the faithful; to be received in faith, and interpreted according to the light that is given. This prime fact of Christian obedience cannot be overstressed.

Our study of the Eucharist takes as its starting point this common ground of Christian obedience to the Lord's command. We shall seek to trace the links by which each particular performance of the one essential eucharistic action is joined invisibly to every other. We shall be led backwards in time to discover as exactly as possible (in a book of small compass) the origin of the Eucharist in the incarnate life of our Lord, and in the Jewish tradition of worship in which he was nurtured. We shall also move forward in time, as we seek to understand the significance of the Eucharist as transcending time, and as bridging the 'gap' between the Ascension and the *parousia*. And we shall be led outwards in space, from our individual experience and the corporate experience of the tradition in which we worship, to try to understand something of the significance of the Eucharist as that which draws together into unity the scattered people of God. At each stage, the link with eternity will be stressed; for this is the link which binds together past, present, and future, here, and there, *into one*. For this reason our first study must be of the High Priesthood of Christ, and his eternal self-offering in the heavenly places.

2

Royal Priesthood

Some sort of apology may appear to be necessary for basing a book about the Eucharist on a study, however brief, of the Epistle to the Hebrews. It may be objected that we should properly begin with an examination of those passages in the gospels which record the Supper of the Lord, not to mention the earlier account given by St. Paul (1 Cor. 11.23-26). The fact is, however, that the exceedingly brief narratives which we have of the Supper are not easy to understand without reference to the theology of the New Testament taken as a whole. To make this assertion is to raise immediately the question whether there is such a thing as 'the theology of the New Testament'. Would it not be more accurate to speak of the theology of St. Paul, of St. John, of the Apocalypse etc.? Modern scholarship would reply that while different emphases and terms may to some extent be peculiar to different writers, there is nevertheless an underlying unity of theological outlook in the books of the New Testament taken as a whole. This fact may be illustrated by a single example, which incidentally is of some importance for our subsequent study.

Among the epistles two stand out above the general mass of occasional writings in that they set out to give a more or less coherent presentation of Christianity.

These are, of course, the epistles to the Romans and to the Hebrews: and moreover it goes without saying that they come from different pens. Each is a finished, and rounded, composition. One is addressed to a mixed community of Jews and Gentiles, living and worshipping in a particular place; the other to a purely Jewish group, or possibly to Hebrew Christians in general. Admittedly their approach is different, their language different, their area of discourse different. Some readers might be inclined to say that these two epistles present almost irreconcilable views of the Christian religion; but, as we shall see in a moment, they are in fact complementary.

The Epistle to the Romans starts from the common predicament of all men, Jew and Gentile alike, without Christ. It faces up to the moral demands of the Mosaic Law, and shows that all men have sinned and fallen short of the righteousness which a righteous God must necessarily demand. St. Paul then goes on to preach salvation, offered freely to mankind, through the death and resurrection of Jesus Christ, who has perfectly fulfilled the righteousness of the Law. He stresses the triumphant faith by which the true Christian lives as an adopted son of God, waiting for final deliverance from the corruption of this world-order 'into the glorious liberty of the children of God' (Rom. 8.21). Finally, after dealing with the problem of Jewish apostasy, he outlines the quality of Christian living in four magnificent chapters (Rom. 12-15). The overall plan of the epistle may be summarized very briefly as follows: (1) Man's predicament, (2) God's way of dealing with it, (3) The result in Christian living. And throughout the epistle the background is morality. St. Paul's thought starts from the manward end, and moves in ethical terms.

The unknown author of the Epistle to the Hebrews starts from the eternal being of God the Son. The first scene, so to speak, is set in heaven. This epistle too faces up to the demands of the Mosaic Law, but it is the ancient law of worship which now occupies the stage. Worship is something which is due from man to God; something which brings man into fellowship with God. This epistle asserts the transitory nature of the Jewish sacrificial system, and indeed the ineffectiveness of all pre-Christian ritual worship. Christ is presented now as the One who offers the one perfect offering for mankind. He is the eternal High Priest, for whom all the heroes of the faith were waiting. The epistle claims finally that we have access in him to the Father, through a sacramental worship which fulfils and also transcends the foreshadowings of the older dispensation. Again, to summarize the plan of the epistle in the briefest possible manner, we have: (1) God the Son, pre-existent in glory, (2) God's provision of the perfect offering, (3) The result, recovered fellowship of man with God. Throughout this epistle the background is worship. The thought starts from the Godward end, and moves in sacrificial terms.

Yet, different as these two epistles may appear at first sight, they are in no sense at variance with one another, and indeed each presupposes the other. The redemption proclaimed in Romans is procured by a sacrificial death, vicariously offered for the ungodly (Rom. 5.8). The failure of the earlier worship, pointed out by Hebrews, lay in the fact that it did not touch the root of ethical action (Heb. 10.4-5). The divine initiative in redemption, and the key position of faith, are given full expression in both epistles. The Incarnation of Christ, and the

B

adoption of Christians, also are common ground. But whereas one epistle places the greatest emphasis on *living* as the sons of God, the other is chiefly concerned with *worshipping* as the sons of God. The two epistles are complementary. Their centres of gravity are in different places; but for a full presentation of the Christian position we need both, equally.

The New Testament basis of our thinking about the Eucharist is therefore to be found in the Epistle to the Hebrews. For our purpose Romans, with its manward emphasis, can largely be taken for granted. Yet Hebrews is a difficult book. It speaks to us in an idiom far removed from our modern way of thinking; and it is only by considerable mental effort that we can enter into its essential message. The necessity for that effort, however, is surely underlined by the fact that the liturgical epistles of Christmas Day, Passion Sunday, and Good Friday are drawn from this book, as well as the second lesson for Evensong on Ascension Day. The principal turning points of the more significant half of the Christian year draw somewhat heavily therefore on the Epistle to the Hebrews.

The starting point, as we said earlier, is the eternal status of God the Son, sharing in true equality with the Father in the essential being of Godhead, far above all created beings, both men and angels. The message begins with the proclamation that God has ' in these last days spoken unto us by his Son, whom he hath appointed heir of all things, by whom also he made the worlds '. The Son through whom he speaks is ' the brightness of his glory, and the express image of his person . . . made so much better than the angels, as he hath by inheritance obtained a more excellent name than they '. (Heb. 1.2-4)

God's act in Christ, the Incarnation, Death, Resurrection, and Ascension, accomplished for our salvation, find succinct expression in a single verse: 'But we see Jesus, who was made a little lower than the angels for the suffering of death, crowned with glory and honour'. (Heb. 2.9) Christ's true status, his condescension, his suffering, and his exaltation, form the opening theme of the epistle. For this writer, God's act in Christ is primary. From the proper grasp of this flows his whole presentation of Christian worship.

To read further, however, we need to understand the concepts of 'priest', and 'king'. In the first instance, historically speaking, both priesthood and kingship are human institutions, or offices, made necessary by the social organization of mankind under God. Yet, as will appear later, both have their origin in God himself. For the present though, we shall regard them as human institutions, of almost universal occurrence in relatively primitive societies. And we cannot help observing that both kingship and priesthood seem singularly remote from our modern organization of society: so vast that it is depersonalized, so man-centred that God is commonly left out of account.

The function of the priest is to represent man before God. In primitive religion man's conception of God may be wholly inadequate, or even false: the activities of the priest unedifying, or even repulsive. The fact remains, however, that in primitive societies, almost without exception, the priest fulfils a necessary function as the Godward representative of the group. And in spite of the fulminations of the Hebrew prophets against the corrupt ritual worship of their own day, we do well to recognize in the concept of priesthood an indispensable element in the approach of mankind to God. The function of the priest is to speak and to act on behalf of man in his relation with God. Man's true relationship with God, his Creator, is expressible only in worship. Man is unable to approach the Almighty except he bring a worthy offering, so expressing the worth-ship of God. Not that God needs what man can offer: it is *man's* need which is met in the act of worship. The unworthiness of the individual, as he seeks to approach to God, makes him desire someone to represent him, to speak and act on his behalf. Again, the fact that the human priest is commonly no more worthy to approach God than are those whom he represents, must not blind us to the true insight which demands the services of a priest. Nor must we ignore the obvious fact that only a man can represent men before God. However imperfectly the ideal is realized in primitive societies, we recognize therefore the necessity of the priest, a man set apart to speak and to act on man's behalf in his approach to God. The work of the priest necessarily includes the expression in words of God's worth, and the offering to God of something of inexpressible value.

The function of the king is to rule, to govern, to be the fount of authority, and the law-giver, within the social group. Not only primitive societies but even European states until quite recent times provide countless instances of kings who were mere despots. The knowledge that kingship can so easily degenerate into despotism and tyranny must not blind us to the fact that a social group invariably requires a focus for its natural patriotism and coherence, and that of necessity that focus must be a member of the group. The Hebrew nation, unique among ancient peoples, came to recognize the conditions under which alone kingship may be exercised in a world of God's ordering. The king must rule and govern in wisdom and righteousness in accordance with the will of God. He must show love and fatherly care for his subjects, in keeping with the revealed nature of God. For in essence, the function of the king is to represent God to men. Again, the fact that no man is worthy to be God's representative must not blind us to the necessity of such a function in human society. Even with Nero in mind, St. Paul could write: 'The powers that be are ordained of God' (Rom. 13.1).

Democratic government has commonly taken the place of the earlier forms of kingship: for man has almost everywhere risen up against the imperfections of kingship as it has been realized in human society. Yet even to-day, all states retain a single person as a focus of authority, so acknowledging this essential element in society. The head of the state may be a constitutional monarch, or an elected president, or even a tyrant who has manipulated the party machine to his own ends. In each case, the person concerned appears to be necessary for national solidarity; and in each case, though perhaps in different degrees, he witnesses to the same essential element in human organization.

The priest, then, represents man to God: the king represents God to man. Priest and king: each is a focus in human society: one in the religious, the other in the political, ordering of the group. But are they necessarily *separate* foci? In an illuminating passage, Bishop Westcott writes, 'He who unites with the Unseen must direct action. He who commands the use of every endowment and faculty must be able to consecrate them. He who represents man to God with the efficacy of perfect sympathy must also represent God to man with the authority of absolute power.'[1] Ideally then we must not think of the two offices as entirely separate; but rather as capable of being combined in a single person; who as priest represents man to God, and as king represents God to man. In one Person only has this ideal been achieved; in Christ Jesus our Lord. In drawing together and fulfilling the diverse strands of messianic prophecy, Jesus uniquely combines both the kingly and the priestly elements. (Kingly, Isaiah 9 and Daniel 7; priestly, Isaiah 53.) The deepest insight, perhaps, of the Epistle to the Hebrews is that it recognizes in the Man Christ Jesus a Royal Priesthood, which fulfils as nothing else can the deepest needs of mankind. He is our Priest by whom we have access to the Father; and he is our King, ruling in our hearts in love and righteousness.

DIVINE SACRIFICE

For the writer of the Epistle to the Hebrews the ideal unity of the two offices of priest and king is foreshadowed in the remote personality of Melchisedec. We need not inquire who this person really was in historical fact. By the time the New Testament was written Melchisedec was simply the personification of that which is predicated of him in Genesis. He was 'king of Salem' and 'priest of the most high God': and we read that he 'brought forth bread and wine', and that he blessed Abram (Gen. 14.18, 19). This strange figure, who apparently combined in his own person the kingship and the priesthood in prehistoric Jerusalem, can be thought of as antedating both the kingship and the priesthood of Israel. Appearing on the scene as it were 'without descent, having neither beginning of

[1] *Epistle to the Hebrews*, 2nd ed., p. 201.

days, nor end of life' (Heb. 7.3), he seems to the writer to typify an eternal royal priesthood, in terms of which the total work and status of Christ can be expressed.

Accordingly Jesus, who is set before us in this epistle as the One in whom priesthood and kingship perfectly coalesce, is described as 'a priest for ever after the order of Melchisedec' (Heb. 7.21). His divine origin from all eternity marks him out as by right exercising kingly authority: just as the title 'Christ' recognizes him as the Anointed One, the One who reigns. When his work on earth is completed, he sits down 'at the right hand of the Majesty on high' (Heb. 1.3); taking again the throne which is his by right; waiting till his enemies are made his footstool, i.e. until his just kingship is universally recognized. Moreover, his life and work on earth, and the manner of his return to the Father, mark him out as the perfection of priesthood. By virtue of his Incarnation he shares perfectly in our human nature and condition. He is one of us. He knows joy and fellowship; privation, disappointment and suffering, as Man. As Man also he knows the force of temptation. He knows man's condition from the inside, so to speak; and such inside knowledge gives him the perfect sympathy (in the full, deep meaning of that much abused word) in which lies the power of redemption. 'In that he himself hath suffered being tempted, he is able to succour them that are tempted' (Heb. 2.18). Yet he is without sin. As perfect Man, he is our perfect Representative before God: and that entirely by the grace of God, who has himself provided the Representative.

Look now how the Epistle to the Hebrews develops the understanding of Christ's Passion, Death, and Ascension as his high priestly work. The Resurrection, we may notice, is not explicitly mentioned. It is the Ascension which is supremely important in the mind of the author, though of course the Resurrection is necessarily implied. A more significant difference of emphasis is the absence of the thought of Jesus as the Lamb of God. Perhaps the phrase suggests something too passive. Instead, Hebrews draws out the meaning of the verse, 'Lo, I come to do thy will, O God' (Heb. 10.7, from Ps. 40.7, 8); so stressing the active side of Christ's redeeming sacrifice, thinking of him first as the perfect Priest, and only after that as the perfect Offering. It is indeed the active work of priesthood which supplies the medium of this brilliant interpretation of Christian redemption.

The writer's experience of priesthood was entirely within the Jewish system. Being a Hebrew, he does not write in terms of general principles, but in terms of the concrete sacrifices with which he is familiar. For the modern reader this limitation, and the consequent attention to the minute details of the sacrificial system, can be a real bar to a sympathetic understanding of the message. The Jewish sacrificial system was undoubtedly the highest thing *of its kind* known to man. Yet to our way of thinking it is in many respects crude; offensive even, to our more delicate susceptibilities. What we have to grasp, in spite of this, is that for its own day and before the coming of Christ it met a real need. And because the Spirit was at work in Israel under the Old Covenant, the sacrificial system expressed true religious insights, and sought to meet the problem of man's approach to God in the only way in which it can be met.

The Jewish sacrificial system, therefore, is preparatory only. It foreshadows and leads up to the perfection of Christ's redeeming sacrifice. The earthly sanctuary is spoken of as a shadow of the heavenly (Heb. 8.5). But the sacrifices offered under the old Law were ritual only (Heb. 10.1-4). They did not, and could not, avail for sin. Moral failure lay outside their proper scope (Heb. 9.9). The sacrifices needed endless repetition, in that there was no perfection, or finality, of achievement. They were therefore ready to be done away, and replaced by something better. Indeed the old sacrifices were already superseded from the moment when the Old Covenant was broken through Israel's disobedience. In 586 B.C. Jerusalem was sacked, and the nation scattered: and though, after the return from captivity, there was a renewal of the old worship, such renewal was outward only. An outworn ritual was awaiting its replacement in God's good time by something which should really meet man's need at the deepest level. The New Covenant had been foretold by Jeremiah (Jer. 31.31-34) in the hour of Jerusalem's calamity, and this prophecy was to be fulfilled in Christ.

Nevertheless, the old Jewish sacrifices, and in particular the ritual of the Day of Atonement, provide a pattern in terms of which the redemptive work of Christ can be expressed. As the Epistle to the Hebrews traces the ritual of the Day of Atonement (Chapter 9), the author is at pains to point out its failure and imperfection. But at the same time he makes full use of the sacrificial concepts, and of the actions of the Jewish high priest, in order to express the perfect work of Christ. Underlying this interpretation of Christ's redemptive work is the ancient concept of the blood as the *life* of the sacrificial victim (Gen. 9.4). It is the offered *life* of the sacrifice which is thought of as possessing cleansing or atoning value. The death of the victim is strictly incidental to the sacrifice, and is thought of only as liberating the life-blood for sacrificial purposes. Yet without the death of the victim the sacrifice would be an impossibility; and to this degree therefore the death guarantees the validity of the offering. Remote though all this may seem from the reality of spiritual religion as we know it within the Christian Church, yet some grasp of these fundamental concepts is necessary if we are to follow the significant line of thought which the Epistle to the Hebrews expresses for all time.

Our Lord Jesus Christ is the true High Priest, who fulfils and transcends all human priesthood under the Old Covenant. His death on the Cross, involving the shedding of his blood, liberates the Perfect Life; which is offered to God, on man's behalf. The spiritual character of the offering is sufficiently safeguarded, if we remember that it is the Incarnate Life which is offered: the Life which had been lived on earth entirely to the glory of God, and which on the Cross was laid down and commended into the Father's keeping. All this, for the writer of Hebrews, is summed up in the concept, 'blood'. Let us now follow through the implications of this sacrificial interpretation of Christ's death in terms of the high priest's ritual action on the Day of Atonement, which foreshadows our redemption.

In the earthly sanctuary, made according to Jewish belief after the pattern of the heavenly, a veil separated the Holy of holies from the usual place of worship; and the ark of the Covenant, overshadowed by the cherubims within the veil, typified the very presence of God. Into this presence nobody but the high priest entered; and that only once in the year, bearing the blood of the sacrifice. The high priest represented the people before God: in his person they were brought into God's presence; and fellowship was renewed, once in the year. 'But Christ being come an high priest of good things to come . . . by his own blood . . . entered in once into the holy place, having obtained eternal redemption for us.' (Heb. 9.11, 12) On behalf of his people, Christ passes through the veil into the true presence of the Father. The reality of Christ's high-priestly work is asserted by the fact that he is *now* in the very presence of God. The Ascension, completing the offering which we sometimes think of as taking place on Calvary, is the guarantee of his high-priesthood. As High Priest, he pleads his perfect offering by his *presence*, by being where he is. Fulfilling and transcending all priesthood, he represents us perfectly to the Father. 'Wherefore he is able also to save them to the uttermost that come unto God by him, seeing he ever liveth to make intercession for them.' (Heb. 7.25) His offering of his own *life*, unlike those imperfect and un-availing sacrifices made under the Old Covenant, is alone able to 'purge our conscience from dead works to serve the living God' (Heb. 9.14).

Moreover, Christ is described as *seated* 'on the right hand of God' (Heb. 10.12, etc.). The contrast is thereby drawn with the earthly high priest who *stands* to offer those imperfect sacrifices 'which can never take away sins' (Heb. 10.11). Christ's work is finished, and complete, and effectual. The fact that he shares the throne of his Father implies that his offering is accepted. Thereafter he reigns as Priest-King, in virtue of his own true kingly status and his high-priestly act now completed on man's behalf. Our author sees a further parallel between the return of the Jewish high priest from the Holy of holies when his ritual is accomplished, and the expected *parousia* of the Lord. Christ having accomplished his perfect offering on man's behalf, as Priest and King will return in the end of the times to receive the submission of all men. 'So Christ was once offered to bear the sins of many; and unto them that look for him shall he appear the second time without sin unto salvation' (Heb. 9.28).

Passion, Ascension, and *parousia* are now linked together in the thought of this epistle, and interpreted as the fulfilment of the divine pattern of salvation which had been foreshadowed in the Jewish sacrificial system. And Christ has not only fulfilled the older ritual by which man sought to come into the presence of God: he has transcended and perfected it in every particular. Where, under the old dispensation, an unwilling animal victim was slain and its life offered by an agent entirely external to itself, the Incarnate Son makes a voluntary offering of himself, laying down his own life willingly for the sin of mankind. Where, under the old dispensation, the life offered was irrational and amoral, the Life now offered on man's behalf is one of perfect human quality, activated entirely by motives of love and obedience to the Will of God. Man is truly represented now—by the Priest, and in the Offering. God has provided himself a Lamb (Gen. 22.8): even more, he has provided Himself a Priest. 'Lo, I come to do thy will, O God. . . . By the which will we are sanctified' (Heb. 10.9, 10). God has done for man what man could never do for himself. In Christ the barrier of sin is broken down. The veil of the Temple is 'rent in twain from the top to the bottom' (Mark 15.38). Man has access to the presence of God; not imperfectly by the representation of a merely human priest standing in the Holy of holies, but in the Perfect High Priest who has passed through the veil and is seated at the right hand of the Father. He who deigned to share our human nature and condition has taken that same human nature triumphantly up into heaven, and in that nature reigns eternally. The Divine Sacrifice has been offered, once for all, and has been accepted. The New Covenant, promised by God through the prophet Jeremiah in the moment of deepest human failure, has been sealed in the blood of the Royal High Priest, who ever liveth to make intercession for us.

LIFE UNDER THE NEW COVENANT

What now is the new status of Christians? We cannot do better than go back to the words of prophecy (Jer. 31.31-34) in order to answer this question. 'Behold, the days come, saith the Lord, that I will make a new covenant with the house of Israel, and with the house of Judah.' The New Covenant, first of all, will reunite the broken people of God. 'Not according to the covenant that I made with their fathers in the day that I took them by the hand to bring them out of the land of Egypt; which my covenant they brake, although I was an husband unto them.' The Old Covenant indeed gave deliverance, in an earthly sense, from the oppressor; but it required an answering obedience to the declared will of God. In this lay its weakness; and the moral failure of the chosen nation inevitably led to the abrogation of the covenant relationship, in spite of the patience and long-suffering of God. 'But this shall be the covenant that I will make with the house of Israel: After those days, saith the Lord, I will put my law in their inward parts, and write it in their hearts; and will be their God, and they shall be my people.' The external obedience, required under the Old Covenant, is to be replaced by a new personal relation-

ship and status which is freely given by God. Law is to
be replaced by grace; mere obedience, by love from the
heart. In this, of course, the Gospel is clearly foreshadowed. The initiative and action are entirely God's.
He will act decisively for the salvation of his people, and
what man cannot do for himself God will do on his
behalf. 'And they shall teach no more every man his
neighbour, and every man his brother, saying, Know the
Lord: for they shall all know me, from the least of them
unto the greatest of them, saith the Lord: for I will for-
give their iniquity, and I will remember their sin no
more.' The new offer of salvation through grace is not
to be confined to the old Israel, but is to be universal. The
barriers between man and man, as well as the barrier
between man and God, are to be broken down by God's
act. Forgiveness of sin is to be offered freely to all men;
all will be drawn into one fellowship of the Spirit; all
will share in the universal gift of God's grace. As another
prophet saw, ' the earth shall be filled with the knowledge
of the glory of the Lord, as the waters cover the sea '
(Hab. 2.14).

All this is fulfilled in the New Covenant of Jesus
Christ: but its fulfilment is infinitely costly. Here again
the concepts of the old sacrificial system serve to express
deep truth which can hardly be expressed otherwise.
' Almost all things are by the law purged with blood; and
without shedding of blood is no remission.' (Heb. 9.22)
There is mystery in the very existence of evil, which
absolutely demands suffering for its expiation. That insight was perceived under the old dispensation; which
expressed it, though inadequately, in ritual form. It was
given its clearest expression in the Suffering Servant pro-
phecies: ' the chastisement of our peace was upon him;

and with his stripes we are healed' (Isa. 53.5). Supremely it is expressed in the New Testament. No sooner was Jesus recognized by his disciples as the One that should come than he began to teach that 'the Son of man must suffer' (Mark 8.31, etc.). A divine necessity seemed to be laid upon him: he must 'give his life a ransom for many' (Mark 10.45). But his suffering is entirely voluntary, caused though it is by the cosmic fact of evil. From the merely human point of view Jesus is put to death; his life is taken. In the deeper view of scripture, he *gives* his life. 'I lay down my life, that I might take it again. No man taketh it from me, but I lay it down of myself.' (John 10.17, 18)

In the thought of the Epistle to the Hebrews, not only is the offering of the blood of Christ the very condition of the bringing in of a New Covenant; it is the condition also of the full perfection of the Redeemer himself. 'It became him, for whom are all things, and by whom are all things, in bringing many sons unto glory, to make the captain of their salvation perfect through sufferings. For both he that sanctifieth and they who are sanctified are all of one: for which cause he is not ashamed to call them brethren.' (Heb. 2.10, 11) Or again, 'Though he were a Son, yet learned he obedience by the things which he suffered' (Heb. 5.8). This concept is by no means easy; for we cannot suppose that Christ's moral perfection was in any way lacking during his earthly life. We should remember, however, that in the Incarnation he united to himself human nature: not a particular human nature, but human nature in its widest sense. He carried that human nature with him through life, and suffering, and death, and resurrection, and ascension, up to the throne of the Father. At each stage Jesus brought human nature

to the appropriate perfection; in a world already torn by
sin, and at enmity with God. In this sense, therefore,
Christ's humanity was made perfect, whole, and complete, through suffering. His full perfection as Man, in
this sense, was reached only after death; when, passing
through the veil and ascending into the heavens, he
brought human nature as God intended it into the presence of the Father.

This insight enables us to understand something of the
new status of Christian believers. Christ brings 'many
sons unto glory'. He is 'the captain of their salvation'.
The Sanctifier and the sanctified 'are all of one'. We are
called his 'brethren'. Our human nature, redeemed by
Christ, is united to his perfect nature. Baptized communicant Christians, who have learned to trust wholly
in the one perfect offering of Jesus Christ, are *made one*
with him. By grace we are brothers of him who is the
only-begotten of the Father. We are given 'power to
become the sons of God' (John 1.12) through the Life of
him who is the Son of God by right.

What is given here and now as a status must become a
moral actuality before we can enter upon our inheritance.
The process of sanctification, by which this is accomplished through grace, goes on throughout the life of
each Christian. Each must be lifted up, in the Spirit and
by grace, into the sanctifying suffering and obedience of
the Son. The actual human nature of each one of us must
be conformed to the perfect human nature of the Son;
and this is effected for each one of us only as the power
of Christ's sufferings and resurrection takes possession of
our very being.

Christ is *par excellence* the Royal Priest. By faith, or—
more accurately—by grace, through faith, (Eph. 2.8)

Christ's Church is privileged to share corporately in that royal priesthood which is his by right. 'Ye are a chosen generation, a royal priesthood, an holy nation, a peculiar people; that ye should shew forth the praises of him who hath called you out of darkness into his marvellous light.' (1 Pet. 2.9) United with Christ, as the members with the Head, we are in him. We share corporately in his sacrificial activity. In so doing we enter upon the sacramental heritage of the Church; and that perfection, that wholeness, which is Christ's, is communicated to us as we learn to participate by the Spirit in his perfect Offering.

3

The Supper of the Lord

The Eucharist takes us back to the evening meal, in the upper room in Jerusalem, on the night before Jesus suffered. The unbroken tradition of Christian worship can certainly be traced back thus far. But what precisely happened at the Supper? That is a question which is much less easy to answer than might be supposed.

We have, of course, more than one account of the Supper in the New Testament. Yet all are exceedingly, even tantalizingly, brief. We are left to fill in all the detail for ourselves from mere hints in the recorded narratives, and from our general knowledge of Jewish custom in so far as it can be reconstructed for the first century. More serious still, the brief accounts which we have are not in complete agreement as regards such detail as they do give.

Before looking at the narratives of the Supper, however, it is important to realize one great difference between these and the accounts which we have of other events in the life of our Lord. During the oral period of the tradition, the majority of the more important events of the Lord's ministry would be narrated frequently in the *teaching* of the faith to new converts; and eventually were committed to writing. Such variations as exist between the different written traditions may be ascribed principally therefore to the inaccuracy of the human memory; and, to a lesser degree, to conscious modification for theological reasons. The Lord's Supper, however, provided the basis and pattern of Christian *worship*. The words spoken by the Lord on this occasion, and the actions accompanying them, acquired almost immediately a liturgical use, and were constantly repeated in a liturgical setting. Liturgy is a living thing; and it is inevitable that any record of the Supper, as it was finally incorporated into the written gospels, should have been coloured by the development of the tradition of worship in the intervening years. Diversity of liturgical tradition in Churches separated geographically (even during thirty or forty years) may account for some of the difference between the several narratives. Yet, of course, it must be emphasized that no effort would be spared to preserve pure and unaltered all that was considered essential in the liturgical tradition.

In the apostolic period, and for some considerable time afterwards, great secrecy surrounded the worship of the Christian Church. Such secrecy may account for a certain reticence, or reluctance, to commit to writing too much detail when the narrative of the Supper came to be recorded in the gospels or elsewhere, lest the written word should fall into the hands of unbelievers. (It is in fact remarkable that we have no extended account of the celebration of the Holy Eucharist before the middle of the second century.) Such accounts of the Supper as are preserved in the gospels and in the first Epistle to the Corinthian church are, therefore, somewhat stylized in language and liturgical in form. They are allusive rather than descriptive; because it could be assumed that the

Christian reader would already be familiar with the details of the meal through his own participation in the liturgy of the Church. Anything more than the barest account of the Lord's words and actions would seem out of place in a matter so sacred. Yet such bare accounts do serve the one essential purpose for which they were written. They place the origin of the liturgy at its correct point in the more extended narrative of the Passion. It was on the night before he suffered that the Lord took bread, and blessed, and brake, and gave it to his disciples. The Christian reader of the first century need be told no more: he knew the rest already, for he was present at the 'breaking of the bread' Sunday by Sunday.

PAUL, MARK, AND LUKE

Of the three independent accounts which we have of the Lord's Supper, that in the first Epistle to the Corinthians was written the earliest, probably A.D. 54 or 55. It bears witness to the tradition of worship which St. Paul imparted to this Church at its foundation a few years earlier. St. Mark's Gospel belongs to the period between A.D. 65 and 70, and is generally supposed to be nearer to the earlier of these dates. Though there had been contact between Mark and Paul on the latter's first missionary journey, their ways seldom coincided after that time. It is generally held that Mark came much more under the influence of St. Peter; and consequently the second gospel provides us with a tradition largely independent of the Pauline teaching. St. Luke's gospel is commonly dated some ten years later than Mark's. The so-called 'we-passages' in the Acts of the Apostles are clear evidence that Luke had worked with Paul for a considerable time; but the third gospel's account of the Supper suggests that Luke had access to other lines of tradition than that embodied in 1 Corinthians. The passion narrative of St. Matthew is so closely dependent upon that of Mark that there is no need for us to treat his account of the Supper separately.

Let us now compare the three independent accounts which we have. We must do this somewhat carefully, however, because we are already so familiar with all three narratives, that we tend unconsciously to read into each all that we associate with the Lord's Supper. We need to be on our guard, and to look carefully for the small differences in detail. These differences will be seen most clearly if we set out in tabular form what each narrative actually says. To this end we shall distinguish four elements: (1) the Lord's *actions*, (2) the *words* which he used in giving the bread, (3) the words of *explanation* which accompanied the giving of the bread, and (4) the Lord's *command* to repeat what he did. The words and action over the cup can then be dealt with in a similar manner. (The Authorized Version is followed. Words in brackets are not found in the Greek text.)

St. Paul (1 Cor. 11.23-26)
Action: ' . . . the Lord Jesus the (same) night in which he
    was betrayed took bread: and when he had given
    thanks, he brake (it),'
Word: '(Take, eat:) this is my body,'
Explanation: ' . . . (which is broken) for you:'
Command: 'this do in remembrance of me.'
Action: 'After the same manner also (he took) the cup,
    when he had supped,'
Word: 'This cup is the new testament in my blood:'
Explanation: None.

Command: 'This do ye, as oft as ye drink (it), in rememberance of me.'

The final verse (v. 26) offers an overall explanation of the rite in Paul's own words: 'For as often as ye eat this bread, and drink this cup, ye do show the Lord's death till he come.' From this follows the apostle's familiar admonition against unworthy reception of the sacrament (vv. 27-29).

St. Mark (Mk. 14.22-25)

Action: 'As they did eat, (Jesus) took bread, and blessed, and brake (it), and gave to them,'
Word: 'Take, (eat): this is my body.'
Explanation: None.
Command: None.
Action: 'And he took the cup, and when he had given thanks, he gave (it) to them: and they all drank of it.'
Word: 'This is my blood of the (new) testament,'
Explanation: 'which is shed for many.'
Command: None.

Mark's account concludes with the Lord's vow of abstinence, 'Verily I say unto you, I will drink no more of the fruit of the vine, until that day that I drink it new in the kingdom of God.'

St. Luke (Luke 22.15-20)

The peculiar characteristic of the third gospel's account is the mention of a preliminary cup before the institution proper, and the Lord's vow of abstinence from all future earthly passovers and from 'the fruit of the vine, until the kingdom of God shall come' (vv. 15-18). Then follows:

Action: 'He took bread, and gave thanks, and brake (it), and gave unto them,'
Word: 'This is my body'
Explanation: 'which is given for you:'
Command: 'This do in remembrance of me.'
Action: 'Likewise also the cup after supper,'
Word: 'This cup (is) the new testament in my blood,'
Explanation: 'which is shed for you.'
Command: None.

It should be remarked at this point that the shorter text of St. Luke, supported by a minority of the manuscripts, breaks off part way through verse 19; that is to say, immediately after the word spoken at the delivery of the bread.

What do we observe now as we set these three independent accounts side by side?

(1) All three are in substantial agreement as regards Christ's action, both over the bread and over the cup. Thus, he took, blessed (or gave thanks), brake, and gave the bread. He took the cup, and gave thanks over it, and gave it to the disciples. Only Mark actually says this in so many words. Paul and Luke clearly imply it by the use of the words, 'after the same manner', or 'likewise'.

(2) The words spoken by Jesus in the delivery of the bread, 'This is my body', are precisely the same in all three accounts, both in English and in Greek. The words spoken over the cup are substantially the same in all three accounts.

(3) Both Paul and Luke record the same words of explanation over the bread, while Mark gives no words of explanation. Paul gives no words of explanation over the cup, beyond what is implied by the reference to the blood

of the new testament (covenant) in the words of administration. The evangelists explain that the blood (which the cup represents) is 'shed for many' (Mark), or 'shed for you' (Luke).

(4) Paul records a command to repeat what Christ did, both with the bread and with the cup. Mark records no such word of command: Luke gives it with the bread only.

In spite of these differences in recording the Lord's words of explanation, or of command, we can say nevertheless that all three authors appear to understand the significance of the total act in the same way. The sharing in the bread and the cup represent the disciples' partaking, in some sense, in the sacrifice of Christ, and in the benefit of salvation so procured. The verbal differences may be due to the omission of words actually spoken by Jesus; or to additions which express something of the spiritual experience of the early Church. But such additions, if additions they are, may be held to be entirely in keeping with our Lord's own understanding of his actions on the night before he suffered. It is perhaps rather surprising that the command to repeat Christ's action is recorded only in three (and omitted in three) of the possible instances. Nevertheless, the fact that the Church did repeat the Lord's action from the very beginning is sufficient evidence how the disciples understood his intention.

The prayer of consecration of the English Rite in common with many of the historic liturgies, draws together all the elements of the tradition into a single narrative: 'Who, in the same night that he was betrayed, took Bread; and, when he had given thanks, he brake it, and gave it to his disciples, saying, Take, eat, this is my Body

which is given for you: Do this in remembrance of me.
Likewise after supper he took the Cup; and, when he had
given thanks, he gave it to them, saying, Drink ye all of
this; for this is my Blood of the New Testament, which
is shed for you and for many for the remission of sins:
Do this, as oft as ye shall drink it, in remembrance of
me.' Thus, for our own generation also, liturgy provides
the form of narrative best known to the worshipper; and
that by conflating the essential elements of the several
accounts to be found in the New Testament. In so doing,
the Church gives expression to the fact that the central
act of Christian worship consists in obedience to the
Lord's command to do this in remembrance of him.
In another chapter we shall look more closely at the
deeper meaning of the phrase, 'in remembrance of
me'. For the present we turn, however, to a different
question.

WAS THE SUPPER A PASSOVER MEAL?

All the gospels make it clear that the Passion of our
Lord took place at the Passover season; but there is no
general agreement as regards the exact chronology of
the events of the Passion relative to the Jewish observance. Even within a single gospel there are apparently
conflicting notes of time, which learned discussion is still
at pains to resolve. Broadly, however, we may distinguish
two traditions: one preserved by the synoptic gospels, the
other by St. John. These are set out schematically in the
Table overleaf.

The rules for the observance of the Passover, as the
annual commemoration of Israel's deliverance out of
Egypt, are laid down in Exodus, chapter 12. 'In the first
month, on the fourteenth day of the month at even, ye

CHRONOLOGY OF THE PASSION

Event	Modern Reckoning	Clock Time	Jewish Reckoning	
			Synoptics	Fourth Gospel
Supper prepared	Maundy Thursday	6.0 p.m.	14 Nisan Preparation	13 Nisan
....			....	....
Supper eaten				
....	....	Midnight		
Arrest Trials Crucifixion Burial	Good Friday		15 Nisan First Day Of Unleavened Bread	14 Nisan Preparation
....		6.0 p.m.	....	....
....	....	Midnight		
	Easter Eve		16 Nisan (Sabbath)	15 Nisan First Day of Unleavened Bread (Sabbath)

shall eat unleavened bread' (v. 18). The Jewish month, of course, is a lunar month, and the Passover takes place therefore at full moon. It will be remembered also that by later Jewish reckoning the day begins at sunset, roughly 6 p.m. In New Testament times, therefore, the lambs were normally killed on the afternoon of 14th Nisan, the day of preparation. The Passover meal was eaten during the night of 14th/15th Nisan, beginning at sunset; and thus 15th Nisan was reckoned as the first day of unleavened bread.

Now the synoptic gospels on the whole appear to support the view that the Supper was the Passover meal. The events of the Passion, beginning with the Supper and ending with the burial, take place according to the synoptic tradition on the first day of unleavened bread. The chronology of the fourth gospel, however, makes the Supper the evening meal of the previous day, the day of preparation, 14th Nisan. According to this tradition the events of the Passion take place entirely on the day of preparation, and the Lord is buried by sunset of that day, just before the feast of the Passover begins. The two chronologies are mutually exclusive. There is no possibility of harmonizing them. Scholars are more or less equally divided in accepting the one or the other as historical. Whichever is the correct tradition, much of the detail of the Passion narrative, in either of its forms, is difficult to reconcile precisely with known Jewish custom. Clearly it is not possible here to enter into the intricacies of this subject. We must be content with the general outline of the tradition of the Lord's Passion, leaving the more difficult historical questions open, and inquiring instead what theological significance attaches to each of its opposing forms.

If for the present we accept the synoptic tradition that the Supper was the Passover meal, we can reconstruct the details somewhat as follows. The Lord as the head of the 'family' of disciples presides at table, and pronounces the familiar blessings over the various courses. The ritual is in fact quite complicated, but presumably sufficiently well known to the original Christian readers of the gospels to need no description. Each ritual Jewish meal opens with the appropriate *kiddush*, at which dishes corresponding roughly to our modern *hors d'oeuvre* are eaten by all present as a preliminary to the meal proper. The passover *kiddush* comprises a first cup of wine, followed by a dish consisting largely of bitter herbs, and fruit juices. The cup is blessed by the head of the family, and shared. This presumably would be the preliminary cup of wine mentioned only by St. Luke. The herbs are interpreted by the head of the family in terms of the Egyptian bondage from which Israel was delivered by God at the time of the Exodus.

Next follows the Passover liturgy, recalling God's blessings and in particular his deliverance of his people. The first part of the Hallel (Pss. 113-118) is then recited, and a second cup is drunk before the principal course is eaten. The main course is introduced by a grace said over the unleavened bread, which is broken by the head of the family. All who share in this bread are thought of as sharing in the Passover blessings. The lamb is eaten in accordance with the provisions of Exodus: 'And they shall eat the flesh in that night, roast with fire, and unleavened bread; and with bitter herbs they shall eat it. . . . And ye shall let nothing of it remain until the morning' (Exod. 12.8, 10). This is followed by the blessing and sharing of a third cup of wine. The whole rite is brought to a close with the recital of the remainder of the Hallel, and the drinking of a fourth cup.

Such was the familiar observance of the Passover in the time of our Lord, and it is possible to see certain clear resemblances to the ritual of the Supper described in such scant detail in the New Testament. As we have seen already, the preliminary cup mentioned by St. Luke may be the *kiddush* cup. Accepting the synoptic tradition, we may identify the bread which our Lord blessed and broke, saying the words, 'This is my body', as the unleavened bread of the main Passover course. The cup which all the narratives record as being blessed and shared, as the Lord spoke the words, 'This is my blood of the new testament which is shed for many', is then the third Passover cup, the cup of blessing. The Lord's apparent refusal to drink of this cup himself is to be linked with the thought of the cup of suffering, which he was soon to drink, by which a redemption greater than that from Egypt was to be wrought, and the Kingdom of God to be brought in.

Indeed the Supper is to be interpreted, on this view, as the Passover meal in which the old ordinance is fulfilled and transcended, and the greater deliverance is inaugurated. Christ himself is the true Passover Lamb, provided by God (Gen. 22.8). In sharing the unleavened bread broken by the Lord, the disciples share in the blessing of Christ's Passover sacrifice of himself. This synoptic view then accords well with the Pauline teaching, 'Christ our passover is sacrificed for us: therefore let us keep the feast, not with old leaven, neither with the leaven of malice and wickedness; but with the unleavened bread of sincerity and truth' (1 Cor. 5.7, 8).

Nevertheless, it is by no means certain that the Supper was the actual Passover meal, plausible though this reconstruction may appear. On the Johannine view the Supper was the evening meal of the disciples with their Lord on the previous day. The crucifixion and death of Christ then take place according to this chronology on the day of preparation. Indeed St. John lays great stress on the fact that Jesus died on the Cross precisely at the hour when the paschal lambs were being slain in Jerusalem in

accordance with the ancient Jewish ritual. Christ the true
Paschal Lamb, ' which taketh away the sin of the world '
(John 1.29), dies at the appointed Passover time. It is
recorded therefore that ' they brake not his legs . . . that
the scripture should be fulfilled, A bone of him shall not
be broken ' (John 19.33, 36): the reference being, of
course, to the regulations of Exodus 12.46. In this fulfilment John sees deep significance, and indeed his whole
Passion narrative appears to hang on the identification
of Jesus with the true Paschal Lamb slain at the very
hour prescribed by the Jewish law.

But in this case, how are we to interpret the act of our
Lord at the Supper, which is now no longer to be
regarded as the Passover meal? The answer is that,
although it is held on the eve of the Passover, the meal
still has a religious character as looking forward to the
feast itself. It was apparently a common thing for a
group of men to bind themselves together into a
chaburah, or fellowship of brothers, for religious purposes. Our Lord and his disciples can be thought of as
forming such a *chaburah*. The Supper is then a normal
chaburah meal, held on the eve of the festival, with its
own well-defined ritual, looking forward to the Passover
itself.

Once again the main part of the meal would open with
the breaking of bread by the head of the family, with a
grace beginning, ' Blessed be Thou, O Lord our God,
eternal King, Who bringest forth bread from the
earth. . . .' The meal would conclude with the blessing
and sharing of a cup of wine, over which the head of the
family had pronounced a similar benediction. It is
suggested that the words of institution, ' This is my body '
and ' This is my blood of the new testament ', were added

to the appropriate graces as the bread and the cup were shared. The Lord's words then give a new significance, to the blessing customary at the *chaburah* meal, which the disciples could not fail to recall whenever they should meet together at supper on future occasions.

In this case, the Lord's words at supper, 'With desire I have desired to eat this passover with you before I suffer' (Luke 22.15), express the fact that he knows that he will be prevented by death from partaking of the actual Passover that year. Yet the significance of the Supper is still to be found in a Passover context, even if it is not itself the Passover meal. From the repetition of the re-interpreted rite, in accordance with Christ's command, the early Eucharist took shape as a weekly fulfilment of the Jewish Passover. And St. Paul could write, 'The cup of blessing which we bless, is it not the communion of the blood of Christ? The bread which we break, is it not the communion of the body of Christ?' (1 Cor. 10.16).

THE NEW COVENANT

Technical questions of exact New Testament history and Jewish ritual observance must now be left on one side. They are of the utmost interest to scholars; and only by their solution can we ever delineate the precise stages by which the Eucharist is derived from the Supper of the Lord. Certainty, however, is at present impossible on many points of considerable interest; and in the absence of agreement on the question of the relation of the Supper to the Passover, we must be content to draw conclusions of a general character.

The Supper took place in the Passover season. Without doubt the Passover was in Christ's mind, as was also his impending death. Clearly the Lord himself, and the New

Testament writers after him, understood his action at
the Supper in terms of his creative fulfilment of the
Passover.

The Lord's symbolic action at the Supper, followed
by his sacrificial offering of his life as 'a ransom for
many' (Mark 10.45), inaugurated the New Covenant
promised by God through Jeremiah. Indeed the symbolic
action with the bread and the cup was actually the beginning of the sacrificial action, which led to Calvary and
culminated in Christ's passing through the veil into the
presence of the Father. When Jesus and his disciples
came together at the Supper, the die was already cast.
Judas had covenanted to betray his Master. Jesus knew
full well that the hour was come in which the Father
would be glorified, and the Son would be glorified in him.
He was ready to offer himself; for his earthly work was
now done. The seventeenth chapter of St. John's gospel
reproduces Christ's high-priestly prayer, expressing
before the Passion his complete dedication to the doing
of the Father's will. From this point there could be no
going back. Yet the agony in the garden, the physical
suffering, the destitution, and the burden of sin, still had
to be borne. The cup must be drunk to the dregs, by
which the New Covenant was inaugurated. And so, inter-
preting his Passion symbolically in advance to his disciples, Jesus gives the broken bread as 'My body which is
given for you'; the cup as 'The new covenant in my
blood which is shed for you'.

The disciples have followed their Lord throughout the
earthly ministry: they cannot follow him now. He must
tread 'the winepress of the . . . wrath of Almighty
God': alone. 'I come to do thy will, O God': alone.
But that redemption, which Christ wrought alone for

man, must be made effectual in the life of each individual believer. The disciples, and all who should come to believe through them, must have a sacramental way by which they can enter into the offering made on their behalf, and in some sense identify themselves with it. Otherwise the Cross would remain something external to the Christian; effectual to a degree psychologically, but not ontologically. The Lord therefore re-interpreted one form of the thanksgiving ritual of the Jewish family, or religious group, so that it became the Eucharist of the Christian Church, the new family of God. This symbolic action, which began the inauguration of the New Covenant, provided also for regular repetition, in order that the benefits of the New Covenant might be made available, and the lives of the faithful knit ever more closely into the covenant relationship in the blood of the Redeemer. All this, and more, is contained in the command, 'Do this in remembrance of me.'

After the Resurrection and the outpouring of the Spirit at Pentecost, the disciples obeyed this command. The Church spread throughout the known world, and thousands were added to its membership. Regularly on the first day of the week, the day of the Resurrection and of Pentecost, the Church assembled to break bread in accordance with its Lord's command. What was its experience? Perhaps we can best answer this question in two short sentences. The Church discovered as a fact of experience that in the breaking of bread it had its own unique act of worship transcending all Jewish forms. And in the wilderness of a hostile world it knew that it was fed by its living Lord.

D

4

Praise and Thanksgiving

Anyone who reads the New Testament straight through from cover to cover cannot fail to be struck by the sharp division which occurs about half-way. The gospels describe the principal events in the public ministry of our Lord, and taken together they give a quite amazingly full historical testimony. Even though critical analysis has narrowed down the area of reasonably established fact, yet we feel we know the general course of events quite fully up to this point. As we read on into the Acts of the Apostles, however, the tempo changes perceptibly. Here we have a book whose purpose appears to be to show how Christianity travelled from Jerusalem to Rome. We are surprised to find that Peter and Paul are the only apostles who play any appreciable part in the narrative, and we are left wondering what the others did. And whereas the gospels devote altogether rather more than one hundred chapters to perhaps three years of history, the Acts devotes less than thirty chapters to more than thirty years of history. The rest of the New Testament is a collection of occasional writings, dealing with particular pastoral or theological problems arising from time to time in the different local churches; and it is only with difficulty that we can fill in a few of the numerous historical gaps.

If we want to know anything about the day-to-day life of the Christians, how numerous they were, how they were organized, or how they worshipped, we are left to read between the lines, and piece together the overall picture as best we may. And it is a somewhat hazardous undertaking, giving rise to a great many minor disagreements among scholars. Certain general impressions, however, we do get, about which there can be no argument. The early Christians were drawn largely from the lower classes of society, with only a sprinkling of wealthy or important people. Although the Jewish dispersion was a contributory factor of some importance to the initial spread of the gospel, we find that the Gentile element quickly came to outnumber the Jewish. Even so, the Christians formed only a tiny minority of the whole population. Indeed, until the third century, their usual places of worship were the private houses of the few better-off members. Sometimes they were able to meet together more or less openly: at other times, periods of persecution drove them literally underground.

In spite of the complete absence of all the normal amenities of church life, the early Christians seem to have been filled with joy and gladness. Words such as 'thanksgiving' and 'blessing' appear on page after page of their writings. The qualities of love, joy, and peace, rub shoulders with long-suffering, and meekness (Gal. 5.22, 23). Quite clearly we have no right to picture human nature in the first century, even among the Christians, as notably more perfect than at other times in the world's history. Yet we do get the impression that little groups of underprivileged and often down-trodden people were living a triumphant corporate life in the Spirit, certain of their new status as the beloved of God, and looking with joy for the return of their Saviour Jesus Christ. Everywhere they were conscious of being the *ecclesia* of God, the New Israel. By their faith in Jesus Christ, and in the power of his resurrection, they had inherited the promises made to the fathers. Small and insignificant though they were in the eyes of men, they were intensely conscious of being God's chosen people in the new age, a royal priesthood in a world that scorned them.

FROM HOUSE-CHURCH TO BASILICA

Let us then try to piece together such glimpses as we have of the earliest Christian worship. We are given one such glimpse in the second chapter of Acts: 'They continued steadfastly in the apostles' doctrine and fellowship, and in breaking of bread, and in prayers . . . and . . . continuing daily with one accord in the temple, and breaking bread from house to house, did eat their meat with gladness and singleness of heart' (vv. 42, 46).

The scene is Jerusalem. The Christians are Jews who have accepted Jesus as the promised Messiah. Their Christianity is the fulfilment of their Jewish religion, which they have not in any sense renounced. They still worship in the Temple and in the synagogues, as their Lord did before them. But the table-fellowship of Jesus and his disciples has expanded to include the new converts. Sharing all things in common the Christian community meets in each other's houses, observing the table ritual of pious Jews. There can be little doubt that the 'breaking of bread' refers to a fairly close repetition of the Lord's Supper. It is commonly held that the first day of the week was marked by such observance from the very first, as a weekly celebration of the Resurrection and of the outpouring of the Spirit at Pentecost.

What is equally certain is that gradually from this beginning the significance of the Lord's specific words over the bread and the cup would impress itself firmly on the minds and hearts of the new fellowship. The meal, which from the first was a religious occasion, had taken on a new significance as a sharing in the blessings of the Lord's redemptive sacrifice. We may assume that the breaking of bread at the beginning of the Supper would now always be accompanied by a recalling of the Lord's words, ' This is my body which is given for you.' The cup of blessing at the end of the Supper would always now be shared after the recalling of the words, ' This cup is the new covenant in my blood.' The common meal, though still a meal in the ordinary sense, came to acquire also a eucharistic significance, in our sense of the words; but there was no immediate separation of the one element from the other. The ' breaking of bread ' was the ' love-feast ' of the Christians, of which the more strictly eucharistic element still formed an intrinsic part.

We get another glimpse of the common fellowship meal some twenty-five years later in the predominantly Gentile city of Troas (Acts 20.7-11). Here was a little Christian community established by St. Paul, and now visited by the apostle on his journey back to Jerusalem. Much more detail is now given, though nearly half of the account is taken up with the record of an accident which befell a certain disciple named Eutychus. Again it was the first day of the week : presumably by Jewish reckoning, and therefore what we should call late Saturday evening. Paul was to leave on the following day; and making the most of his short time in Troas, preached until past midnight.

Still the assembly meets in an upper room, belonging

we may suppose to a wealthy member of the congregation. (St. Paul's epistles sometimes convey greetings to prominent Christians, mentioned by name, adding 'with the Church that is in their house'.) Here in Troas we read that 'there were many lights in the upper chamber, where they were gathered together'. Even as long ago as this, the lamps, necessary as they were, had also a religious significance. There is evidence that the Christian Church long continued the ancient Jewish custom of the blessing of the lamp, which came to have an added significance as representing Christ the Light of the World. The actual Supper in Troas follows the preaching of the word in the small hours of the morning, and in its turn is followed by general conversation, as we should expect, before the apostle departs. 'When he . . . had broken bread, and eaten, and talked a long while, even till break of day, so he departed.' Still the Christian fellowship meal and the specifically eucharistic observance form a single whole. But here in Troas we have a congregation which is predominantly Gentile. Now there is no sharing in the worship of the Temple: possibly none in the local synagogue. Separation of the Christian and Jewish elements is becoming inevitable. The breaking of bread is beginning to take its place as the specific act of worship of the Christian community, distinguishing it from all others. Preaching, fellowship, communion, and praise, all find their place in this one single act, as we have seen.

It appears, however, that development was not so smooth, and conditions not so happy, in the newly-founded Church of Corinth. Indeed it was the very abuses which accompanied Christian worship in that city which provided the occasion for St. Paul's only recording of the tradition of the Lord's Supper (1 Cor. 11.23-26). There had been heresies and divisions; some claiming to follow Paul, some Apollos, some Cephas (Peter), and yet others setting themselves up as a 'no-party' party, claiming to follow Christ (1 Cor. 1.12). Gross breaches of the moral law had occurred. Fellowship was threatened, and the weekly celebration of the Supper had been turned into an occasion of gluttony and drunkenness.

Paul was constrained to write, 'When ye come together therefore into one place, this is not to eat the Lord's Supper. For in eating every one taketh before other his own supper: and one is hungry, and another is drunken' (1 Cor. 11.20, 21). The better-off members, with time on their hands, had already turned the Supper into a common feast, before the poorer, hard-working, and hungry members were able to be present. Under these conditions the supper is no longer the Lord's Supper at all. Nobody must suppose that in taking part ritually in such an observance he is sharing in any sense in the blessings of Christ. Rather are these members eating and drinking damnation to themselves, 'not discerning the Lord's body' (1 Cor. 11.29). The apostle therefore lays down the rule that anyone who is hungry must satisfy his hunger at home first, before coming to the Lord's Supper: an interim arrangement, apparently, for he concludes, 'the rest will I set in order when I come' (1 Cor. 11.34).

We seem to detect in Corinth the beginning of a movement which resulted ultimately in the complete separation of the Eucharist proper from the general fellowship meal of the Christians. During the next two centuries the love-feast, or *agape*, developed entirely as a separate institution; a kind of charitable supper, held in the houses of the well-to-do, to which friends were invited. It became a private meeting of a group, rather than the assembly of the Church as such. Food was still blessed, usually by a cleric if one was present: but the meal was in no sense the Eucharist. Both Eucharist and *agape*, it is true, had their origin in the ritual Jewish meals, in which the Lord had shared with his disciples. For the Jew every meal had a religious significance, and was eaten with thanksgiving to God, who had provided the good things of the earth. But as the Church moved out into a Gentile world, where this religious background did not exist, it was only natural that the original combined observance of Supper and Eucharist should be abused. Their separation not only did away with the opportunity of abuse, but also made possible the independent development of the Eucharist as the supreme corporate act of worship of the Christian Church.

Before tracing further the development of eucharistic worship, it will be convenient at this point to give some account of its normal setting in the larger houses of Christian people throughout the Graeco-Roman world. Until almost the time of Constantine, Christian worship was essentially a private affair; often conducted in the greatest secrecy, especially during periods of persecution. The Eucharist was a corporate domestic act, taking place in the hall or *atrium* of the great house, around the table which was still used on other occasions for ordinary meals. The bishop, without whom the Church was not complete, sat in the place of honour facing the congregation across the table. Around him on either side sat his fellow clergy, the presbyters; and the deacons assisted in the distribution of the elements.

It is generally agreed that the imagery of the vision of heaven described by St. John the Divine owes a great deal to the contemporary earthly setting of Christian worship, with which the seer was familiar. 'Behold, a throne was set in heaven, and one sat on the throne. . . . And round about the throne were four and twenty seats: and upon the seats I saw four and twenty elders sitting, clothed in white raiment.' (Rev. 4.2, 4) The worship offered by angels, living creatures, and elders, through 'the Lamb that was slain', affords a glimpse of the significance which already was attached to the Christian Eucharist. 'Blessing, and honour, and glory, and power, be unto him that sitteth upon the throne, and unto the Lamb, for ever and ever.' (Rev. 5.13) The known and familiar setting of the Eucharist in the house-church of the first century is transformed in St. John's vision into heaven itself; somewhat as the Temple setting of the older sacrificial worship had been transformed for the prophet Isaiah in the day when he experienced his call (Isa. 6). In St. John's vision the eternal God, seated upon the throne of heaven as the true Father of the family of the redeemed, receives the worship and praise of all creation; the worship and praise which the earthly father-in-God offers up in the Eucharist on behalf of all the faithful. But more of the liturgy later: our concern now is with the setting of Christian worship in the early days, not with its form.

During the third century here and there, and in the fourth century almost universally, the changing status of the Christians in Roman society brought the Eucharist for the first time out into the open. Churches were built, and sometimes lavishly endowed and equipped. The natural conservatism of the Church, and the need for continuity in liturgical expression, brought about the adaptation of the secular basilican type of building to Christian use. Such a building consisted of a rectangular

hall, with the entrance at one end, and a semi-circular
apse at the other. The bishop's throne occupied the central position against the wall of the apse. In front of it
stood the altar, simple, square, and unadorned: on either
side, following the curve of the apse, the seats for the
elders. The general congregation occupied the body of
the hall. Orientation was by no means as rigid as it was
to become in later centuries; and it is probable that in the
majority of Churches the bishop still celebrated the
liturgy facing the congregation across the altar no matter how the building lay.

In something like three centuries a transformation had
come over the worship of the Church. As long as the
Christians remained a sect of Jewry, they continued to
attend normal Jewish worship; and the breaking of bread
remained a domestic religious observance, latent with
possibilities, but still undifferentiated and undeveloped.
Two major changes had to take place before the simple
fellowship meal based on the Lord's Supper could develop
into the central act of worship of the universal Church.
The first of these changes was the separation of the *agape*
from the Eucharist proper: an adaptation necessitated by
the different circumstances of the Gentile world. The
agape persisted for a while as a separate institution, but
eventually more or less died out. It ceased to serve a necessary purpose in Christian society. The other major
change was the liberation of the Christian Church from
the constant fear of persecution, once its numerical
strength and spiritual vitality had secured for it the
recognition and respect of the secular authorities. Called
out into the open, with a vocation to the whole world,
the Church readily adapted its previously domestic
worship to meet the needs of society at large. The relative

simplicity of the private house gave place to the magnificence of the basilica. The bishop, previously unknown except to his little flock, became the spiritual leader of a whole city's life. The Catholic Eucharist became the universal expression of worship, as the civilized world was conquered for Christ.

PRIMITIVE LITURGY

If the New Testament and the Christian literature of the next hundred years tells us little about the manner in which the Eucharist was celebrated, there is an even more remarkable reticence over the prayers which were said. We do know that in the earliest days considerable liberty was allowed to the celebrant as regards the spoken word. Liturgy is a living thing; and it was only by slow degrees that relatively set forms of prayer developed and secured adoption in particular regions. Even so, the variations from locality to locality were probably as wide as those obtaining between the separated 'churches' of to-day. To this degree of variation differences of temperament and geographical isolation contributed not a little. For instance, to judge from material of a somewhat later date, it seems that Eastern forms tended to be elaborate both in content and in expression; while in the West, and particularly in Rome, we find a greater precision and economy in the use of language. Underlying this great outward variation, however, there appears to have been a theological unity, such as can hardly be said to exist to-day between the separated 'churches'.

We have to remember, however, that the Eucharist is primarily an *action*: the corporate response of the Church to the command, '*Do* this in remembrance of me'. The liturgical prayers were originally therefore somewhat brief; their function being solely to express the meaning of the eucharistic action. As we have seen, the eucharistic action comprised two distinct acts or groups of acts, one involving the bread and the other the cup, separated in the earliest times by the main course of the Supper. When the *agape* was allowed to develop as a separate institution, the action with the bread and the action with the cup were brought together. The simplest conceivable form of the rite would therefore be as follows:

The celebrant *took* the bread, *blessed*, *brake* and *gave* it: then he *took* the cup, *blessed*, and *gave* it.

This arrangement, derived directly from the Lord's act at the Supper, has been called the 'seven-action-shape' of the liturgy. There is no evidence that it persisted for any appreciable period. Indeed the earliest tradition recoverable witnesses to a simplification of this, giving rise to the so-called 'four-action-shape', as follows:

The celebrant *took* the bread and the cup, *blessed* them, *broke* the bread, and *gave* the bread and the cup.

This arrangement became the classical shape of the liturgy, presumably on account of its administrative convenience; and has persisted unchanged throughout the greater part of Christendom. The English Rite unfortunately obscures it by directing the breaking of the bread before the blessing of the cup: but even so, much of the economy of the classical shape has fortunately been preserved.

The Eucharist proper expressed the meaning of this

fourfold action from very early times in the great eucharistic prayer, or *anaphora*, spoken by the bishop immediately after an opening dialogue between celebrant and people. If we may take the so-called Apostolic Tradition of Hippolytus as an example, the following represents the practice of the Church of Rome not later than the beginning of the third century:

> The Lord be with you.
> —And with thy spirit.
> Lift up your hearts.
> —We lift them up unto the Lord.
> Let us give thanks unto the Lord.
> —It is meet and right.

We give thee thanks, O God, through thy beloved son Jesus Christ, whom thou didst send to us in the last times to be a saviour and redeemer and the messenger of thy will; who is thy inseparable Word, through whom thou madest all things, and in whom thou wast well pleased. Thou didst send him from Heaven into the Virgin's womb; he was conceived and was incarnate, and was shown to be thy Son, born of the Holy Spirit and the Virgin; Who, fulfilling thy will and preparing for thee a holy people, stretched out his hands in suffering, that he might free from suffering them that believed on thee.

Who, when he was being betrayed to his voluntary suffering, that he might destroy death, break the chains of the devil, tread Hell underfoot, bring forth the righteous and set a bound, and that he might manifest his Resurrection, took bread and gave thanks to thee and said: TAKE, EAT: THIS MY BODY WHICH IS BROKEN FOR YOU. Likewise also the cup, saying: THIS IS MY BLOOD WHICH IS SHED FOR YOU. AS OFT AS YE DO THIS YE SHALL DO IT IN REMEMBRANCE OF ME.

Wherefore we, being mindful of his death and resurrection, do offer unto thee this bread and this cup, giving thanks unto thee for that thou has deemed us worthy to stand before thee and minister as thy priest. And we beseech thee that thou wouldst send thy Holy Spirit upon the oblation of thy holy Church; and that thou wouldst grant it to all the saints who partake, making them one, for fulfilment of the Holy Spirit and for the confirmation of their faith in truth; that we may praise and glorify thee through thy Son Jesus Christ, through whom be glory and honour to thee, to the Father and to the Son with the Holy Spirit in thy Holy Church, both now and for ever. Amen.[1]

In this order, which represents a stage in the development of the liturgy of the Western Church, we may notice the following points:

(1) The prayer is addressed to the Father, and takes the form of a thanksgiving (*eucharistia*), for all his mercies and more particularly for the redemption of the world by our Lord Jesus Christ.

(2) It includes a narrative section, describing the Lord's action at the Supper.

(3) The elements of bread and wine are formally offered to the Father in thankful remembrance of Christ's death and resurrection (*anamnesis*).

(4) The prayer concludes with the petition that the Holy Spirit may come down upon this oblation, in order that the Church may receive the benefits of Christ (*epiclesis*).

(5) The doxology, or ascription, by which the whole eucharistic prayer is offered in Christ to the eternal Trinity.

The breaking of bread, in order that it may be shared, follows immediately; and the service ends with the

[1] H. Bettenson (ed.), *Documents of the Christian Church*, pp. 106-7.

general communion of clergy and people in their due order.

Alongside its eucharistic worship the primitive Church seems to have developed a form of worship of a totally different character, and based ultimately upon the prophetic tradition of the synagogue. The *synaxis*, or assembly, as it was called, consisted of readings from the Scriptures alternating with the recitation of psalms, and ended with a sermon and prayers. The subsequent development of the *synaxis* took place along two different lines: one leading to the Divine Office, the other to an introduction to the Eucharist. Thus, our modern services of Mattins and Evensong are descended from this primitive source by way of the daily hours of the monastic life; and what we would call Ante-communion is derived from the same original source. The fusion of the *synaxis* with the Eucharist took place largely in the fifth century, though naturally the development occurred at different times in different places.

The result then, after about five centuries of liturgical growth, was a form of eucharistic worship which any Christian to-day should be able to recognize. It opened with psalmody and a litany; continued with variable prayers and liturgical readings, drawn from the Old Testament, the Epistles, and the Gospels, alternating with psalmody; and led up to the Sermon preached by the bishop. This first half of the service closed with prayer for the Church and for the needs of its members. The second half comprised the action of the Eucharist: the *anaphora*, or great eucharistic prayer, and the communion of the faithful. The two halves of the liturgy are sometimes referred to as the Mass of the Catechumens, and the Mass of the Faithful, respectively: a reminder that while the catechumens, and even the general public, were admitted to the first part, only the faithful were allowed to take part in the Eucharist itself.

In the performance of the Liturgy all orders of the faithful had their parts to play. It was emphatically not a monologue by the celebrant, as it so often became in later centuries in the West. The very word 'liturgy' means the work of the *laos*, the work of the people of God. Within the wholeness of the worshipping Church, the liturgy of each order of the faithful was an essential contribution. The sermon and the great eucharistic prayer belonged to the bishop. This was his essential liturgy which was seldom, if ever, delegated. At the one Eucharist the assembled presbyters frequently joined with the bishop, however, in the recital of the eucharistic prayer. (Naturally, therefore, arose the custom of a presbyter taking over the bishop's liturgy in the 'daughter' churches as the diocese expanded.) The Gospel was read by a deacon, and the Epistle by a sub-deacon. The deacons led the worship of the congregation, pronounced the dismissals, and administered communion to the faithful. The laity too had their own liturgies, which included the psalmody and the responses. Each person present brought his own offering of bread and wine, from which the elements necessary for the communion were taken, the remainder being used for poor-relief. Indeed the Liturgy was in every sense the corporate act of the whole Church; and it was unthinkable that it should be otherwise.

CORPUS CHRISTI

We have referred to the Eucharist as the *corporate act* of the whole Church. It may be well to pause for a moment to consider the meaning of this phrase: for in spite of its etymology it is so often diluted to mean little more than an act which is performed by one person in the presence of other people. Such is the individualism of the present-day world!

The Eucharist is the corporate act of the Church first of all in the sense that if the liturgy of any single person is missing, the worshipping Church as a whole is maimed: in the same way as a human body from which a limb is missing is maimed. The worship of the Church is not just the simultaneous worship of a lot of isolated individuals who happen to be in the same building. It is the worship of a single whole, a body in which each member plays the part for which he is fitted by God. The thought of the Church as a body, in fact as the Body of Christ, is expressed most fully in the twelfth chapter of the first Epistle to the Corinthians; summed up in the verse, ' Now ye are the body of Christ, and members in particular' (v. 27). It is commonly overlooked, however, that the metaphor of the body is used first by St. Paul not in this chapter, but two chapters earlier, when he is writing about the Eucharist. 'For we being many are one bread, and one body: for we are all partakers of that one bread' (1 Cor. 10.17). Two facts of importance may be inferred from this verse. The concept of the corporate unity of the Church arises in the context of eucharistic worship: and it is the direct consequence of a sacramental sharing in the one bread broken for our salvation.

To put the matter in another way: at the Supper Jesus interpreted the bread and the cup in terms of his own sacrifice, which when complete would inaugurate the New Covenant. The bread of the Eucharist symbolizes his body offered for the sin of the world, the body within

E

which he came to do the perfect will of the Father. To partake of that eucharistic bread is to be identified in the Spirit with his perfect sacrificial offering. We are baptized into Christ's death. We rise with him to newness of life. We are made one body with him through participation in the Spirit in his perfect sacrifice on our behalf. By partaking of him we live in him; and time and again our life is renewed in him. It is for this reason that Christian initiation, begun by baptism, is complete only in first communion. The Church which meets to celebrate the Holy Eucharist is therefore already one body in Christ, because each of its members has already been incorporated into his life. And through partaking again in that corporate act, culminating in sacramental communion, its unity with its Lord is ever renewed and deepened.

Therefore, just as Christ 'the high priest of our profession' offers himself eternally by being in his ascended manhood in the very presence of the Father in the heavenly places; so the Church, which is mystically the Body of Christ, sharing in his royal priesthood, is lifted up through its eucharistic worship into the presence of the Father. In Christ the Church knows its perfect means of approach to the Father, by its participation in the one perfect offering of the Head. And to approach to the Father *is* to worship.

5

The Bread of Life

Although St. John's gospel contains no account of the Institution of the Eucharist, it is by no means lacking in a deep understanding of this great Christian mystery. From first to last the Incarnate Lord is portrayed as 'the Lamb of God, which taketh away the sin of the world' (John 1.29), the One who offers to the faithful disciples eternal life through perfect union with himself. It is well also to remember that in the washing of the disciples' feet at the Lord's Supper, the fourth evangelist describes a parabolic action which expresses the self-giving of Christ as effectually as do the accounts of the Institution in the synoptic gospels. And as if to compensate for the absence of explicit eucharistic teaching, this gospel draws out more fully the meaning of the feeding of the five thousand, and gives us the long discourse on the Bread of Life.

The narrative of the feeding of the five thousand, told in the sixth chapter, is of course well known. Here we need only notice certain points which appear, however indirectly, to give it a eucharistic reference. The fourth evangelist tells us that the event took place about the time of the Passover. The mention of the Passover brings before the mind not only the annual sacrificial meal commemorating God's deliverance of his people under

Moses, but also the far greater deliverance realized by
Christ's voluntary offering of himself at another Passover
season. The people, we are told, had followed Jesus into
the wilderness, whither he had withdrawn with the
twelve for rest and prayer. This wild untamed region
was always something of a terror to the Jew. Yet here, in
the wilderness, the gospel was preached; and it was as
though the prophecy of the messianic age was fulfilled:
'The wilderness, and the solitary place shall be glad; . . .
the desert shall rejoice, and blossom as a rose. . . . The
eyes of the blind shall be opened, and the ears of the deaf
shall be unstopped. . . . And the ransomed of the Lord
shall return, and come to Zion with songs and everlasting
joy. . . .' (Isa. 35.1, 5, 10.) Then bread, in quantity wholly
insufficient by human standards, was offered to the Lord,
and accepted by him. Jesus blessed the bread with thanksgiving, and the people were fed in the wilderness. The
fragments were carefully gathered together, twelve stout
basketfuls; and by some at least of the throng the significance of the miracle was recognized. 'This is of a truth
that prophet that should come into the world.' The feeding of the hungry in the context of the preaching of the
gospel is, and always has been, a 'sign' of the Messiah.
But the sign points beyond itself to the great eucharistic
reality.

The people desired to 'take him by force', half-
recognized but fundamentally misunderstood, 'to *make*
him a king'. He *is* a King, in his own right, having come
down from the Father's side. To escape from the crowd
in the gathering darkness Jesus went up 'into a mountain himself alone'. The disciples started to row back to
Capernaum; and the sea, ever a symbol of man's separation from God, 'arose by reason of a great wind that

blew'. When they were at their furthest from land, Jesus came to them 'walking on the sea'. They were afraid; until they heard the Lord's voice, 'It is I.' Reassured, 'they willingly received him into the ship: and immediately the ship was at the land whither they went', as though in fulfilment of the words of the psalm: 'So when they cry unto the Lord in their trouble: he delivereth them out of their distress. For he maketh the storm to cease: so that the waves thereof are still. Then are they glad, because they are at rest: and so he bringeth them unto the haven where they would be' (Ps. 107.28-30). So often, after gospel and sacrament, the ark of the Church is in stormy waters: but Jesus is not absent, and the ship is in perfect safety in his keeping.

DRAW NEAR WITH FAITH

The discourse which follows the sign of the feeding in the wilderness is the exposition of the first of the great 'I am . . .' sayings of the fourth gospel. It is not strictly eucharistic; but is concerned rather with that basic faith in Christ which underlies our approach to him in the sacrament. In what follows we will seek to draw out something of the meaning of the discourse, so that we may relate the Lord's claim to its fulfilment in the Eucharist.

The people have sought Jesus for the wrong reason, and are warned first of all: 'Labour not for the meat which perisheth', in which there can be only earthly satisfaction, 'but for that meat which endureth unto eternal life, which the Son of man shall give unto you.' Still misunderstanding, they fasten on to the word 'labour', rather than on to the word 'give'. The common Jewish failure to accept God's free offer of salvation is bound up with their preoccupation with 'works', and is

summed up here in the question, 'What shall we *do*, that
we might *work* the works of God?' In reply, Jesus seeks
to deflect their thoughts away from 'works', which can
never win salvation, to 'faith', which is all God asks. Yet
he meets them where they are, by using their own concept: 'This is the work of God, that ye *believe* on him
whom he hath sent.' For his audience, seeing is believing.
They immediately demand a sign, in order that they
may believe. Moses, they say, gave their fathers 'manna
in the desert; as it is written, He gave them bread from
heaven'. But Scripture is misinterpreted if the manna is
supposed to establish the ultimate spiritual authority of
Moses; for it was not Moses who gave 'that bread from
heaven'. Nevertheless the Father, who at the first
deliverance provided manna, now gives 'the true bread
from heaven; for the bread of God is he which cometh
down from heaven, and giveth life unto the world'. The
language of 'works' and 'signs' has now been transcended; and the gift of God (to the world, and not to the
Jews only) is set forth as a Person; who, because he gives
life, can be spoken of under the figure of bread. (John
6.26-34)

The Lord's claim is now made explicit. 'I am the bread
of life: he that cometh to me shall never hunger; and
he that believeth on me shall never thirst.' Jesus himself
is the sign; but they do not believe, even though they
have seen. Faith is not there. Divine election is a mystery.
Yet, 'all that the Father giveth me shall come to me' in
faith. For those that come to Christ, the basis of faith is
the fact that he alone perfectly does the Father's will.
(Cf. Ps. 40.7, 18 and Heb. 10.8-10.) Such faith, though
itself the gift of God, is rewarded by the experience of
eternal life, here and now; and more fully in the world

to come; for Christ promises, 'I will raise him up at the last day.' (John 6.35-40)

If Christ's claim is now explicit, the Jews' objection is made explicit also. They 'murmured at him, because he said, I am the bread which came down from heaven.' A heavenly origin is unacceptable to them, apart from faith; because they can point to his earthly parents. This is a red herring, and Jesus replies by repeating with even greater clarity that 'no man can come to me, except the Father . . . draw him'. Again he renews his promise to 'raise him up at the last day'. The prophets have indeed prepared the way for Christ's teaching. Now Jesus himself declares the whole truth of God, whom no man 'hath seen . . . save he which is of God'. On the basis of this intimate knowledge, given only to the Son, he calls for belief in himself, which alone can confer eternal life. 'Verily, verily, I say unto you, He that believeth [on me] *hath* eternal life', for 'I *am* that bread of life.' The manna in the wilderness was earthly food, and those who ate it are dead. The bread which Christ offers will nourish eternal life here and now. 'If any man eat of this bread, he shall live for ever: and the bread that I will give is my flesh, which I will give for the life of the world.' The bread of eternal life is Christ's own perfect humanity offered to all men, and for all men, irrespective of race. (John 6.41-51)

The cost of the gift is already becoming apparent; and Jesus' reply to the incredulous wrangling of his opponents now makes clear that the cost is death. With calculated emphasis he goes on, 'Verily, verily, I say unto you, Except ye eat the flesh of the Son of man, and drink his blood, ye have no life in you.' The separation of flesh and blood in this context implies the sacrificial death of the speaker. Apart from Christ's complete self-offering through death there can be no 'life'. But to those who believe in the efficacy of that offering, taking it to themselves as very food and drink, eternal life is already a present possession, and the resurrection is assured. This is the very conversion of life, the transition from 'works' to 'faith'. To eat the flesh of the Son of man and to drink his blood, in this context, is to have absolute saving faith in his perfect sacrifice: so that his humanity, perfected through suffering, is indeed the 'meat' of the soul; and his life, poured out unto death, is 'drink indeed'. The believing disciple and the living Lord are mutually knit together: their lives interpenetrate: aspiration is joined in faith to perfect achievement. 'He that eateth my flesh, and drinketh my blood, dwelleth in me, and I in him.' The living relationship between Christ and the Father is reproduced between the disciple and the Lord. And the quality of the life which is given is eternal, timeless, and independent of physical death; because Christ himself lives 'by the Father', who sent him to be the salvation of the world (John 6.52-58).

The gospel of 'life through death', so characteristic of the fourth evangelist, has now been set forth; clearly, though in a figure; and that violence of opposition, which continued to make it a stumbling-block, is already apparent. Even the disciples themselves find the truth almost too hard for their present faith in their Master. Jesus asks, 'Doth this offend *you*? What and if ye shall see the Son of man ascend up where he was before?' Those at least who continued with Jesus, even in spite of their difficulty in grasping the truth, would finally be given vindication of the core of the gospel. For Christ's return to the Father at his ascension is the proof, the authentication, of his claim to be 'the bread of life which came down from heaven'. The word that Christ speaks now, as he walks *incognito*, is to be trusted absolutely, even if it is only imperfectly understood. Outward appearances, which might seem to deny its truth, are to be discounted. 'It is the spirit that quickeneth; the flesh profiteth nothing: the words that I speak unto you, are spirit, and are life' (John 6.60-63).

Does the Lord find faith? At this profound level, faith is possible only as the response to the Father's initiative. 'No man can come unto me, except it were given unto him of my Father.' The inevitable division takes place. 'Many of his disciples went back, and walked no more with him.' Yet there is also a real response of faith, which Peter expresses on behalf of all true disciples: 'Thou hast the words of eternal life. And we believe and are sure that thou art that Christ, the Son of the living God.' One of the twelve still holds back: and Jesus knows it. In the mysterious working of providence the hardening opposition of this false disciple is allowed to be instrumental in bringing about the death on the Cross; by which death is overcome, and eternal life made available to all the world (John 6.64-71).

FULFILMENT

To eat the flesh of the Son of man and to drink his blood is to accept Christ by faith; to feed on him spiritually, by faith with thanksgiving; to be nourished by his life; to live in him. During his earthly life Christ called men to him, and drew them into this intimacy of relationship with himself. But the conditions of the incarnate life necessarily limited the range of his personal contact and influence to a small group of men in one small

nation. The opposition of men when confronted with
perfect goodness brought Jesus to his Cross, and became
the means through which the limitations of the incarnate life were transcended. Risen, ascended, and glorified,
though no longer visible to the little group of men who
had known him on earth, Christ became available to the
faith of all men. In the discourse on the bread of life
Jesus had said, 'no man can come to me, except the
Father which hath sent me draw him.' This is eternally
true: but before he suffered he was able to add, 'I, if I
be lifted up from the earth, will draw all men unto me'
(John 12.32). The growth of the Christian Church after
the gift of the Spirit at Pentecost was the fulfilment of
this promise.

The series of events from the Passion to the Ascension, by which Christ passed through the veil into the
presence of the Father and offered his perfect sacrifice,
is also the series of events by which his influence became
universal, and his offer of eternal life became available to
all men. The eucharistic act, by which Christ interpreted
his self-giving before he suffered, is the means whereby
the blessing of Christ is made available to his Church
most intimately throughout all ages.

The eucharistic experience of the Christian Church
from the very beginning was the experience of an intimate union with Christ personally and corporately: personally, because all experience is ultimately at the
personal level; corporately, because Christ is known in
community and fellowship with other Christians at the
same table. 'The cup of blessing which we bless, is it not
the *communion* of the blood of Christ? The bread which
we break, is it not the *communion* of the body of
Christ?' (1 Cor. 10.16) St. Paul's words can only mean

that the celebration of the Eucharist re-creates the table-fellowship with the Lord, which the disciples knew at the Supper. Then, he was visibly present amongst them: in the Eucharist, he is present to faith. Then, they had fellowship with an earthly Master: in the Eucharist, we have fellowship with the living Lord triumphant over death, and seated at God's right hand. Then, fellowship was in some degree incomplete, owing to the bodily existence of both disciples and Lord: in the Eucharist, fellowship is immediate, complete, and intimate, because the bodily condition imposed by the Incarnation is now transcended.

The means of this intimate fellowship with the living Lord is the partaking by faith of the bread broken in his name, and the cup blessed in remembrance of him. In the Eucharist we are nourished with the bread of which the Lord has said, 'This is my body'; we are refreshed with the wine of which he said, 'This cup is the new covenant in my blood.' Even now in this life, we have in Christ a direct experience of that eternal life which is the fruit of the New Covenant. In such sacramental feeding and refreshment, faith cannot fail to find the fulfilment of the words of the same Lord recorded in the fourth gospel. 'He that cometh to me shall never hunger; and he that believeth on me shall never thirst. . . . I am the living bread which came down from heaven: if any man eat of this bread, he shall live for ever: and the bread that I will give is my flesh, which I will give for the life of the world. . . . For my flesh is meat indeed, and my blood is drink indeed. He that eateth my flesh, and drinketh my blood, dwelleth in me, and I in him' (John 6.35, 51, 55, 56). Nor can faith fail to know, once again in the eucharistic mystery, that the Lord's words of promise are to be trusted absolutely, even if only imperfectly understood. Once again outward appearances are to be discounted; for 'it is the spirit that quickeneth; the flesh profiteth nothing' (John 6.63).

The doctrine of the real presence of Christ in the Eucharist is the necessary corollary of our Christian experience of communion with the Risen Lord; for it is manifestly impossible to have fellowship with one who is absent. The manner of the presence, however, is by no means a simple matter; and unless terms are carefully employed the New Testament faith in the Lord's presence is apt to be conceived in a way which is either too gross or too nebulous. Such definition and elucidation, in so far as it is possible in dealing with so great a mystery, must be attempted in a later chapter. Here, however, we merely assert the incontrovertible fact (incontrovertible, that is, for Christian faith) that in every valid celebration of the Holy Eucharist there is of necessity a fulfilment of the promise: 'Where two or three are gathered together in my name, there am I in the midst of them' (Matt. 18.20). Of one thing we can be absolutely certain: that the Lord is faithful to his promise. In the Eucharist we meet our Risen Lord, and are fed by his life.

6

The Marriage Supper of The Lamb

Two of the Lord's parables, both well known, liken the Kingdom of God to a banquet. There are sufficient resemblances, and sufficient differences, between the two to keep the biblical critics guessing for a long while whether St. Matthew and St. Luke have recorded two independent parables, or two traditions of the same original. For our purpose it matters little; since it is perfectly clear in either case that the Lord made use of the comparison of the Kingdom with a banquet. This is primary. And so far as secondary details are concerned, we may well believe with the majority of the commentators, that the parable of the Great Supper (Luke 14.16-24) reflects an interest in the Gentile mission; whereas the parable of the Wedding Feast (Matt. 22.1-14) reflects a Jewish setting, and an insistence on moral demands as the condition of Church membership.

The figure of the messianic banquet may be traced to its source in Old Testament prophecy, where we read, 'And in this mountain shall the Lord of hosts make unto all people a feast of fat things, a feast of wines on the lees, of fat things full of marrow, of wines on the lees well refined. . . . He will swallow up death in victory; and the Lord God will wipe away tears from off all faces' (Isa. 25.6, 8). Or again, 'Wisdom hath builded her house, she hath hewn out her seven pillars: she hath killed her beasts; she hath mingled her wine; she hath also furnished her table. . . . Come, eat of my bread, and drink of the wine which I have mingled' (Prov. 9.1, 2, 5). This eschatological expectation of the banquet of the Messiah was already in the mind of the guest who remarked somewhat piously, 'Blessed is he that shall eat bread in the kingdom of God' (Luke 14.15); and so prompted the parable of the Great Supper, with its stern note of the rejection of the invited guests, and its offer of universal participation to those outside the covenanted race.

From the point of view of realized eschatology the table-fellowship of Christ and his disciples is already the fulfilment of the prophecy, and an endorsement of the imagery of the Old Testament. Yet the rejection of the invited guests is not complete until Christ himself is finally rejected by the Jewish nation, and sent to his Cross and Passion. Nor does the universal invitation of the gospel of the Kingdom become fully operative until the Lord is risen and ascended. The relevance of Isaiah's words, 'He will swallow up death in victory', then becomes fully apparent; and the eucharistic renewal of the table-fellowship of the Lord then becomes the fulfilment here and now of the Great Feast of the parable. Even so the meaning of the Lord's words is very far from being exhausted. The weakness of the theology of realized eschatology is that it commonly ignores the final consummation of history, and therefore has nothing to say of the perfect fulfilment of all prophecy in the world to come; whereas the Revelation of St. John the Divine bids us look beyond this present world-order to the perfect union between Christ and his Church, when all will be fulfilled. There, using the figure of the Church as the

Bride of Christ, and the ascended Christ as the Lamb, the final goal of history is expressed in the vision of the marriage supper of the Lamb. 'Alleluia: for the Lord God omnipotent reigneth. Let us be glad and rejoice, and give honour to him: for the marriage of the Lamb is come, and his wife hath made herself ready. And to her was granted that she should be arrayed in fine linen, clean and white: for the fine linen is the righteousness of saints. And he saith unto me, Write, Blessed are they which are called unto the marriage supper of the Lamb.' (Rev. 19.6-9)

The pious guest had spoken too easily. Blessed indeed will be those who 'eat bread in the kingdom of God', but before that Kingdom can come in its fulness the warfare of Christ, and the warfare of his Church, must be carried through to final triumph. It is this realization which gives the extra dimension to the eucharistic worship of the Church on earth, and the deepest meaning to the Lord's own abstinence at Supper on the night in which he was delivered up to death.

NEW IN THE KINGDOM OF GOD

All the synoptic accounts of the Supper bear witness in somewhat cryptic language to the Lord's self-imposed vow of abstinence. St. Luke alone records the saying at the beginning of the meal, 'With desire I have desired to eat this passover with you before I suffer: for I say unto you, I will not any more eat thereof, until it be ful-filled in the kingdom of God' (Luke 22.15, 16). The exact meaning of these words is far from clear: we do not even know certainly whether the meal at which they were spoken was the passover supper, or a fellowship meal on the previous day. Hence the Lord may simply be

renouncing all passover suppers after this one, which he
has desired to eat, and is eating. This interpretation, however, seems improbable. Or, he may mean that he will
not eat this Passover, though he is present at its celebration; or again that he knows that he will not live to share
in the Passover even of this year. In any case, however,
one thing is clear. He will not take part in any subsequent
celebration of the Passover until the Kingdom is come.
And this understanding of his words implies that voluntary laying down of his life, which is of the essence of
the Passion of our Lord.

All three synoptic gospels also record a somewhat
similar saying over a cup of wine. In St. Luke, it is said
over the preliminary cup: 'I will not drink of the fruit
of the vine, until the kingdom of God shall come' (Luke
22.18). In St. Mark, it is said over the eucharistic cup:
'I will drink no more of the fruit of the vine, until that
day that I drink it new in the kingdom of God' (Mark
14.25); and this saying over the eucharistic cup is reproduced with only slight verbal alteration in St. Matthew.
The same uncertainty whether or not the Supper is a
passover meal renders exact interpretation a matter of
great difficulty. Nor is it entirely clear that the Lord did
not partake of the cup at the Supper, though this may
reasonably be presumed. All that can be said with certainty is that he knows that he will not again partake on
earth; and he consequently looks forward to the fulfilment of his desire in the coming Kingdom of his Father.

Although considerable uncertainty surrounds the exact
interpretation of these two sayings, conclusions of a
general character may be drawn; and these are highly
relevant to an understanding of the relation between the
Kingdom and the Eucharist. We have seen already that

Christ interpreted his own death as the event which would establish the New Covenant. This is implicit in the words which he spoke over the bread and the cup: 'This is my body': 'This cup is the new covenant in my blood.' And the sacrificial character of the death, so interpreted, is implicit in the separation of the flesh (body) and the blood (life). The Passover was the annual remembrance of the Old Covenant, as well as a partaking in its benefits. The replacing of the Old Covenant by the New therefore not only abrogates the old sacrificial meal, but necessitates the institution of a new observance to take its place. Thus, for the Christian Church the Eucharist replaces the Passover. Indeed Jesus himself is the true Paschal Lamb. The Lord, of course, was fully aware of this, and consequently, so far as he was concerned, the Passover was already abrogated. The disciples were not aware, and could not yet be aware, that the Passover was to be done away. Hence they are to eat it; though (perhaps) Christ abstains.

The New Covenant is a new relationship between God and the true Israel, who accept Christ as Lord and Saviour. It is the basis of our status as Christians. But it is not ultimately *our* status that counts. The status of God is all that matters ultimately. God is King. The recognition and establishment of his complete sovereignty is the goal of all history. Consequently, the thought of the Kingdom of God takes by far the most significant place in the gospels. The Lord's preaching begins with the proclamation of the Kingdom as a present fact. 'The time is fulfilled, and the kingdom of God is at hand: repent ye, and believe the gospel' (Mark 1.15). Nearly all the Lord's parables teach some essential truth about the Kingdom: and indeed the main burden of his preaching in the

F

synoptic tradition concerns the nearness of the Kingdom, the conditions of entry into it, and the blessings which flow from it.

Now we must be careful to distinguish three stages in the coming of the Kingdom. (1) During the Lord's ministry, the Kingdom is present among men, though hidden from the majority. It is proclaimed. Men press into it. Yet the disciples are taught to pray, 'Thy kingdom come'. (2) The Kingdom comes in a fuller sense, with power, during the lifetime of many of those who heard the Lord's preaching. 'Verily I say unto you, . . . there be some of them that stand here, which shall not taste of death, till they have seen the kingdom of God come with power' (Mark 9.1). In the light of St. Paul's description of Christ as the One who is 'declared to be the Son of God with power . . . by the resurrection from the dead' (Rom. 1.4), we can hardly doubt that this second stage in the coming of the Kingdom is inaugurated by Christ's death, and resurrection, and ascension. (3) Nevertheless the Church continues to pray, 'Thy kingdom come'; for it is only too obvious that the recognition and establishment of God's complete sovereignty is still far from complete; even in our own hearts. Not until the end of all things will this goal be attained. But in the meantime, Christ 'must reign, till he hath put all enemies under his feet'. After this 'cometh the end, when he shall have delivered up the kingdom to God, even the Father; when he shall have put down all rule and all authority and power' (1 Cor. 15.24, 25). The period of the Church's warfare leads up to the final establishment of the Kingdom.

In speaking as he did at the Supper, Jesus was quite clearly looking to his own death, and resurrection, and ascension as the decisive events which would bring in the Kingdom 'with power', and would also be the guarantee of the ultimate recognition and establishment of the supreme rule of God. Although, therefore, Jesus interpreted his death to his disciples in terms of the New Covenant and the sacrificial meal which should take the place of the Passover in the New Israel, his own thoughts were fixed on the triumph of the Kingdom. In laying down his own life for the salvation of mankind, he was looking to the complete fulfilment of his work in the consummation of the whole historical process. It is surely this understanding which gives point to the saying, 'I will drink no more of the fruit of the vine, until that day that I drink it new in the kingdom of God.' At the time that Jesus is speaking, the future is foreshortened. To the Lord's prophetic vision, the coming of the Kingdom is seen as imminent. For in the one sense, the end is already about to be realized in the Passion–Resurrection–Ascension event; and yet in another, the end is still to be realized as the distant goal of the historical process.

This foreshortening of the future is typical of prophetic vision at all times. The eschatological fulfilment of prophecy is ever characterized by the holding together of a present reality, known here and now, with the same reality to be known fully in the world to come. Eternal life, fellowship with Christ, the Kingdom of God, we have seen already to be of this character: present realities, to be known in their perfection and fulness only in the future. The same is true of the table-fellowship of the Kingdom. Here and now, in the Eucharist we are given a true renewal and fulfilment of the earthly table-fellowship of the Lord. Yet the Eucharist looks forward to its perfect fulfilment, of which it is now an earthly foretaste. The Eucharist is the fellowship meal of the Kingdom here and now: the marriage supper the perfect fellowship meal when the Kingdom is delivered up to the Father.

Another of the Lord's sayings at the Supper now seems to fall into place. 'I appoint unto you a kingdom, as my Father hath appointed unto me; that ye may eat and drink at my table in my kingdom, and sit on thrones judging the twelve tribes of Israel.' (Luke 22.29, 30) The Church, and of course the apostolate in particular, is called to share in Christ's royal priesthood. The Kingdom is his; but he gives to them a share; so reproducing between himself and his disciples the relationship which exists between the Father and himself. The privileges, which are to be shared, are expressly stated as judgement and table-fellowship, in Christ's Kingdom. There is, of course, a sense in which this promise is fulfilled on earth as the apostle, or after him the bishop, exercises his pastoral and liturgical functions within the Church. But the promise must also look to a future fulfilment in the world to come. It is only in the consummation of all things that the apostles receive their crowns, and the faithful their white robes; that all may share eternally in the worship of heaven, and in the marriage supper of the Lamb.

From our Lord's own lips, therefore, we learn to find our fellowship with him here and now, in the Kingdom which has already come 'with power', by our sharing in the eucharistic feast. But we learn also that we must look beyond our present experience to a reality only dimly discernible to the human mind, when that fellowship will be taken up into perfect union, and we too may drink the fruit of the vine new in the Kingdom of God.

TILL HE COME

The history of God's saving acts on behalf of sinful man falls naturally into three phases. The first is preparatory. It opens with the call of the chosen people, beginning with faithful Abraham; and leads up to the fulfilment of prophecy in the coming of the Christ. The second is the short period of the earthly life of Jesus; culminating in the Passion, Death, Resurrection, and Ascension; and concluding with the promise of the *parousia*, or second coming of the Lord at the end of history. 'This same Jesus, which is taken up from you, . . . shall so come in like manner . . .' (Acts 1.11). The third phase is the period of the Christian Church, during which the faithful wait for the return of the Lord. 'But of that day and that hour knoweth no man, no, not the angels which are in heaven, neither the Son, but the Father' (Mark 13.32). In this third phase, we have fellowship with the Lord. Here and now we are partakers of eternal life in him. But the fulness of those experiences is not yet. Indeed we have a double citizenship: we are called to be *in* this world, but not *of* it: for our true 'citizenship is in heaven' (Phil. 3.20).

The eucharistic worship of the Church is to be seen in this setting. It belongs essentially to an interim period, between the Ascension and the *parousia*. It looks back to the saving act of God in Christ, which culminated in the Passion–Resurrection–Ascension event. It draws its meaning here and now from the perfect sacrifice offered eternally by Christ in the heavenly places. It provides the occasion for the participation of the Church on earth in the worship of heaven; and for the nourishing of the Church on earth with the life of the world to come. By it our true citizenship is renewed and deepened. But the eucharistic worship of the Church here and now looks forward to the *parousia*, when the Lord will return in judgement and in healing, and will make all things new.

When we considered the narratives of the Supper (p. 33) we deferred the interpretation of the Lord's command, 'Do this in remembrance of me.' We are now in a position to draw out something of the meaning of these words: and in doing so we shall link them with the over-all interpretation of the Eucharist with which St. Paul concludes his account of its institution: 'For as often as ye eat this bread, and drink this cup, ye do shew the Lord's death till he come' (1 Cor. 11.26). The biblical word translated 'remembrance' is *anamnesis*, a word which the Church has subsequently used to denote the sacrificial aspect of what is done in the Eucharist (p. 54). The word used by St. Paul and rendered in the English Bible as 'shew', comes from the same root as the word commonly translated 'gospel', and means 'declare', 'proclaim', or 'shew forth'. When, therefore, the Church meets to celebrate the Eucharist, it is for the *anamnesis* of its Lord, i.e. for the recalling of him in the context of worship. By the eucharistic act his death, and resurrection, and ascension are proclaimed, 'till he come'.

The Eucharist is therefore an act of witness before God, and to ourselves. It proclaims the saving history, in this interim period between the Ascension and the *parousia*; and it claims for the Church corporately the benefits of that saving history. That is to say, the eucharistic act, which by Christ's command recalls his perfect offering to the Father, claims the new status which man has in the sight of God by virtue of that offering.

Now it is perfectly clear that an act which recalls a

sacrifice is in some sense sacrificial. In making this assertion we must be careful not to take away anything of the
once-for-all character of Christ's own perfect sacrifice.
Our study of the Epistle to the Hebrews, as well as our
experience of the uniqueness of Christian salvation, alike
warn us that there is precisely nothing that man can add
to Christ's perfect self-offering, by which alone we have
access to the Father. Nevertheless, we must not overlook
the consequences of our incorporation into the ascended
manhood of Christ our Saviour. Nor must we ignore the
depth of meaning in the New Testament claim that the
Christian Church shares in the royal priesthood of Jesus
Christ. ' Ye also, as lively stones, are built up a spiritual
house, an holy priesthood, to offer up spiritual sacrifices,
acceptable to God by Jesus Christ.' (1 Peter 2.5)

The priesthood, to which these and similar words refer,
is not of course a priesthood possessed or exercised by an
individual. It is something essentially corporate. It is
only as individual ' stones ', built up into an organic unity
which exceeds the sum of its parts, that the members
have any share whatever in the priestly function. It is
the Church that is priestly. And the Church shares in a
corporate priesthood because, and only because, the
Church is the Body of Christ, who is himself the ' high
priest of our profession '. For this reason (if for no other)
we cannot suppose that the meaning of the priestly language applied to the Church is exhausted by pointing
either to the moral lives of its members, or to their vocal
offerings of praise. The priestly work of the Church is
necessarily something which the Church *does* as a corporate entity; just as the priestly work of Christ is something which he *does*, as our Representative before God.
Nor is the priestly work of the Church separable from

the priestly work of its Lord. Its offerings are spoken of as 'spiritual sacrifices, acceptable to God *by Jesus Christ*'. What is meant, therefore, is a spiritual sharing as a corporate entity in the one perfect offering of Christ by which we have access to the Father. Just as Christ offers himself eternally to the Father in the heavenly places, simply by being there; so we corporately in him recall on earth, and proclaim before the throne of heaven, that same perfect offering, in virtue of which we share here and now in the life of the world to come.

In this sense the Eucharist is a sacrificial act. But it is an offering wrought out with symbols. The bread, of which Christ said 'This is my body', is the symbol of his perfect humanity in the setting of the eucharistic worship which he instituted. The cup, of which Christ said 'This is the new covenant in my blood', is the symbol of his life-blood shed for our salvation, and recalled in the same context of eucharistic worship. The Eucharist is, therefore, a symbolic sharing in the one perfect sacrifice of Christ, by corporate participation in the symbols which he appointed. The Church as the Body of Christ shares eucharistically in his self-giving act; and corporately in the benefits secured thereby.

For all who partake by faith this corporate sacrificial act, performed in union with Christ's own self-offering, has far-reaching and intimate consequences. The central fact of Christ's symbolic interpretation of his own sacrifice on the night before he suffered, was that he *took* bread, *blessed*, and *broke* it, and *gave* to his disciples. We have been called by Christ to be one bread, one body, with him. In the context of the Eucharist, and in the life which we live in him and for him in the world, this same four-fold action is repeated. We too are taken by Christ;

blessed, in order that we may be made worthy of him; broken, in order that we may lose our self-sufficiency entirely in him; and given back, in order that we may be used ever more intensely to the glory of God the Father. Corporately, and individually, this is the meaning and the effect of our eucharistic sharing in Christ's perfect self-offering. It is the aspect of sacrifice which is expressed supremely in the English Rite: 'And here we offer and present unto thee, O Lord, ourselves, our souls and bodies, to be a reasonable, holy, and lively sacrifice unto thee.' What we must never overlook, however, is that our lives are offered to the Father only in union with the all-sufficient offering of Christ himself, of which the whole eucharistic action is a sacrificial recalling (*anamnesis*), with symbols of Christ's own appointment.

In the world of sacramental reality the Eucharist necessarily effects that which it symbolizes. The self-oblation of the Church in union with its Lord is a sacramental and spiritual self-identification with Christ's own perfect offering through the things that he suffered. Only as the Church identifies itself with its Lord in his perfect humanity by this conscious act of the will does it share in his blessedness. We have seen already (p. 57) that the Church knows itself to be the Body of Christ primarily in the context of its eucharistic worship. In this same context the union of the members with the Head is constantly renewed and deepened, 'until Christ be formed in you' (Gal. 4.19). In the fellowship meal of the Kingdom, each separate life is brought ever more fully under the sovereignty of Christ by the operation of divine grace. In this way by its sacramental participation in the Body of Christ, the Body itself is built up; 'till we all come . . . unto a perfect man, unto the measure of the stature of

the fulness of Christ' (Eph. 4.13). And in each Eucharist
the ontological reality of our ultimate destiny is effected
in the sacramental order; and we taste, as it were transiently, the future blessedness which is prepared for those
who love the Lord in sincerity and in truth. Around the
Father's table we are made sons within the life of the
only-begotten Son. It is in the context of our eucharistic
worship that we cry 'Abba, Father', and that the fulness
of meaning of the Lord's prayer is made real. 'The Spirit
itself beareth witness with our spirit, that we are the
children of God: and if children, then heirs; heirs of
God, and joint-heirs with Christ; if so be that we suffer
with him, that we may be also glorified together' (Rom.
8.16, 17).

So the Church on earth worships 'till he come'. The
new dimension of Christian life is opened up. And 'the
glory which shall be revealed in us' (Rom. 8.18) is seen
here and now as the marriage supper of the Lamb is
anticipated in the Holy Eucharist. With the Church of
all the ages, waiting for the *parousia*, we echo the prayer
of the seer: 'Even so, come, Lord Jesus' (Rev. 22.20).

7

Is Christ Divided?

The fellowship which is experienced within the Christian Church is not a natural quality of human society; but a supernatural gift, of which the giver is our Lord Jesus Christ. As we have seen already, it is known primarily within the eucharistic worship of the Body of Christ; and from there flows out into the life of the Church in its wider activities. So new was this experience that the early Church found it necessary to adopt a special word, *koinonia*, of which the root meaning is partnership, or sharing, in order to express the particular quality of fellowship which it came to know in Christ. The early house-churches testify to the intimacy of the new Christian society; and we are tempted to suppose that within each small circle there existed a closely-knit fellowship in love, which was never ruffled by the petty jealousies which so often disturb human relations. The actual may indeed sometimes have approached to the ideal: but not always, by any means.

The opening chapters of the first Epistle to the Corinthians are evidence for the existence within the local Church of what to-day we should call 'cliques': little groups of people enjoying among themselves a caricature of Christian fellowship, which was based, not on the unity given by Christ, but on common interest or common prejudice. Each had an axe to grind: each was content to be separate from the whole: each supposed itself to be the exclusive possessor of the truth. It is in the nature of a splinter-group to splinter still further. Logically the end is reached when the individual stands alone in self-imposed isolation: and this is hell.

By contrast, Jesus Christ came to bring the Kingdom of heaven: the fellowship based not on individualism but on a common loyalty to a king. In the truly Christian society, the self and its selfish desires are submerged in the common interest of the whole, because each member is obedient to the Head. The Church and the Kingdom of course are not precisely the same thing; though they are closely linked, and cannot be sharply differentiated. Perhaps the safest distinction which we can make between them is to say that the Church is the society of the redeemed, while the Kingdom is the relationship between God and those whom he has redeemed. But clearly in practice Church and Kingdom go very closely together; and the character and progress of both is set before us prophetically in the group of parables which make up the thirteenth chapter of St. Matthew's gospel.

The parable of the Sower speaks of the work of Christ, who sows the good seed of the gospel. A harvest is intended; and a harvest there will be. The succeeding parable of the Tares points equally emphatically to the work of the enemy. The activity of the evil one will be tolerated until the last day. Next follow two parables illustrating rapid growth from small beginnings: the Mustard Seed and the Leaven. Yet each contains also overtones suggestive of the evil which persists even within the Kingdom itself. In Jewish imagery the 'fowls of the air' commonly suggest evil powers; while leaven is almost synonymous with the insidious influence of evil. The extremely terse parables of the Hid Treasure and the Pearl of Great Price are intended to teach the inestimable value of membership of the Kingdom; compared with which all other desirable things are as nothing. The last in the series, the parable of the Dragnet, leaves no room for doubt that the Kingdom will comprise a very mixed multitude, both good and bad, until the final discrimination takes place at the day of judgement.

Altogether this is a not inaccurate forecast of the general course of Christian history. There has been, and will be, a harvest. Evil is nevertheless at work. Wheat and tares grow side by side. The gospel has been preached throughout an ever-widening area; and in certain periods, at least, growth has been enormous. Yet evil individuals find shelter, sometimes gaining great power and prestige within the Church. The subtle poison of wickedness works insidiously, resisted only by the gospel of the Cross, which the world takes to be weakness. Good and bad exist together side by side until the great separation takes place. The criterion then will not be goodness or badness in any abstract philosophical sense; but the attitude of each to the Lord himself, which can be known only to God.

As we contemplate the course of Christian history in the whole spectrum of its life from a St. Francis to a scheming ecclesiastic, from a hard-working slum parson to a time-serving eighteenth-century pluralist, we are tempted to think that the great separation is easily made, and is indeed already a foregone conclusion. Church reformers of all kinds in their consuming zeal for righteousness seem to be temperamentally disposed to

misunderstand the obvious meaning of the phrase,
'known only to God'. The teaching of the New Testament nowhere gives us the slightest authority to make
the distinction between a visible and an invisible Church.
Still less does it endorse the right of a Calvin to distinguish sharply here and now between the elect and the
damned. Nor can any man presume to say that he is
saved. The plain truth is that all who are within the
Church are in the way of salvation. In the literal sense of
St. Paul's words, we are 'being saved' (1 Cor. 1.18). We
are one company, good and bad and not too good all
together; one company within which the gracious influence of Christ is at work, sometimes seen, sometimes
not seen. Many will be saved. Some may ultimately refuse
salvation, and be lost eternally. But within the historical
process the issue remains fluid. Undoubtedly the work of
evil is there to be seen, and some of us see it clearly
enough: but repentance is still open, and ultimate salvation is still available to all.

Within this complex, the spiritual power of evil makes
subtle use of personal animosities and individual pre-
judices. Yet the Spirit witnesses ceaselessly to the truly
Christian ideal of humility, penitence, and love, in fellowship. The power of evil fans natural misunderstandings
of the truth, turning even the eucharistic mystery into
material for disagreement and division. What began far
enough back in history as mere differences of emphasis,
or complementary aspects of the truth, have been twisted,
over-defined, dogmatically asserted or denied, till they
have become permanent matters of acrimonious debate
among Christians. Succeeding generations, nurtured on a
lop-sided theology through no fault of their own, have
been blind to those aspects of truth tenaciously held by

other groups. Time and time again, misunderstanding and prejudice in matters theological, coupled with the desire for power and privilege, when faced by a reforming zeal not over self-critical, have broken the one fellowship given by Christ to his Church. Schisms, once made, are usually beyond human repairing, and tend to become part of the permanent ecclesiastical landscape.

What guarantee is there that we in our generation are wiser than our forefathers? From our position within the web of history, inheriting the mistakes of the past and adding to them our own, what is there that we can do towards the realization of the Christian ideal of visible unity and fellowship? One answer to our question is to insist that unity and fellowship are God's gift to his Church, and consequently only he can give back what man has lost. This is true, in the last analysis. But it is also true that the way back is even now being prepared by the Spirit of God, who is once more brooding upon the face of the waters. And in this way back man has his own part to play: a receptive rather than an active part, but still essential. There are in fact three facets to our human contribution: *First,* that individual listening to the still, small voice which must precede all programme-making. *Second,* clear charitable statement to one another across the barriers, of the truth as we see it, to which our own tradition bears witness. *Third,* a conscious attempt by all the separated bodies to recover the primitive wholeness, both of doctrine and of worship; not in any antiquarian interest or spirit, but in the interest of truth, unity, and fellowship; going back along our several paths to the point at which they diverged.

Bearing in mind these three facets of the human contribution, we must now look very briefly at three

important matters which loom large in our tragic disagreements about the sacrament of unity. They are the
doctrines of the Real Presence, and of Sacrifice, and the
question of Church Order. Each one of these has been
a constant source of disunity within the Body; and the
last-mentioned the human rationalization, though not
the cause, of schism.

THE REAL PRESENCE

At the end of Chapter 5 we insisted on the reality of
Christ's presence in the Eucharist, both as the primary
fact of faith-experience, and as the fulfilment of his own
promise, 'Where two or three are gathered together in
my name, there am I in the midst of them' (Matt. 18.20).
What do we mean when we assert that Christ is present
amongst us? The first step in our discussion is to clarify
further the phrase 'Body of Christ', distinguishing its
several meanings. The word 'body' is itself extremely
rich in meaning. Fundamentally it denotes the outward
organic aspect of the whole man; the physical embodiment of his personality. Hence it comes to mean that
through which a person expresses himself, and gives himself in fellowship, and is known and recognized in fellowship. When we speak of the Body of Christ every one
of these senses is in mind; yet there are four distinct
meanings to the term, according as our attention is
fixed upon the several phases of the Lord's redemptive
activity.

The *natural* body of Christ was a body of flesh and
blood similar to our own bodies, and subject to similar
limitations; in that by his Incarnation God the Son had
accepted our human nature and condition to the full, sin
only excepted. In this body he lived his earthly life and

ministered in the gospel. Yet we must surely agree that the natural body of the Lord was no more than a transitory condition of the Incarnate life; in so far as the human body is subject to the vicissitudes of this created order. In his natural body Christ suffered, was crucified, and was buried. On the third day the tomb was empty.

After the Resurrection Christ was known to his disciples; and we may justifiably speak now of his *spiritual* body, as the seat of his being or embodiment of his personality. The gospel tradition testifies plainly that during the forty days following the Resurrection, the Lord was able to clothe himself visibly in accordance with his own will and purpose, in order that he could communicate with his disciples, and be recognized by them. But now, risen from the dead and ascended into heaven, Christ has completely transcended the limitations of an earthly mode of existence. Accordingly we are driven to use symbolic language in speaking of the Lord's present state; and this we do when we make the credal affirmation that 'he sitteth at the right hand of the Father'. In the strict use of language we must assert that limitation of location, characteristic of earthly existence, is transcended. If Christ is 'in heaven', yet we know that he is also still available to faith, on earth; without limit of location, and invisibly. Everywhere he is available to the faith of his disciples; but more especially in the Eucharist, where his specific promise is honoured. Our difficulties in understanding the doctrine of the Real Presence begin to be resolved once we learn to think of Jesus as present invisibly in his ascended manhood as the true Celebrant of every Eucharist. He comes to us in his spiritual body, in order to receive our love and homage,

G

to feed us sacramentally, and to draw us into deeper fellowship with himself and with one another. And our experience of Christian fellowship brings us to think of the Church as the *mystical* body of Christ.

The *mystical* body of Christ is the whole company of the faithful: militant on earth, expectant in paradise, and triumphant in heaven. The mystical body is organically united with the Risen and Ascended Christ; owns him as its Head; and is nourished by his life. In the Eucharist, as we have seen, the Church shares in Christ's perfect self-offering to the Father. It is sent out from worship to work: to be his hands and his feet; to carry the gospel of love by word and deed to those who do not know him. When called to suffer at the hands of the world, it suffers in union with its Head, filling up 'that which is behind the afflictions of Christ' (Col. 1.24); because mystically it is his Body.

The fourth sense in which the term 'Body of Christ' is used relates to the reality by which Christ communicates himself to us in the sacrament: his *sacramental* body. This in fact is the only sense in which the Lord himself spoke of his body; and, of course, he used the word in a deeply symbolic sense. When the mystical body is assembled for worship, with its Ascended Lord present in his spiritual body as the true Celebrant, the faithful are fed and refreshed with the mystic gifts of bread and wine, consecrated by thanksgiving to God in his name. So Christ gives himself to the faithful by means of his sacramental body. We receive him into our hearts by faith, with thanksgiving and with adoration. The words, 'This is my body', 'This cup is the new covenant in my blood', are the ultimate guarantee of the real presence of the Lord among his disciples: spiritually, mystically, and sacramentally. What a tragedy it is that such deep truth should ever have been affirmed or defended in such a way as to provoke its virtual denial! And yet this is precisely what has happened in the past five centuries of Christian history.

Typical of the gross misunderstanding of the eucharistic reality, which there has been to our shame on either side, is the so-called black rubric of the Book of Common Prayer; itself a violent reaction against the crudities of medieval popular religion. Yet if this rubric is read in the light of the distinctions of meaning which we have just tried to express, it will be seen to rest on the most complete confusion of thought. Here at least in the interest of understanding and reverence, it is essential that we should get behind the medieval and reformation periods; and seek to recover something of the wholeness of primitive belief, without the embarrassment of over-definition.

A source of serious misunderstanding in some quarters is the Catholic teaching that a sacrament is valid *ex opere operato*. This does not mean that the effects of the sacrament are produced 'automatically' in the communicant, irrespective of a right attitude of reception, and irrespective of a humble faith. Such a view is properly rejected by Protestant theology. What is meant is that, provided the Eucharist is celebrated in communion with the historic Church, Christ is faithtful to his promises. The bread, of which he says, 'This is my body', is his sacramental body, by which the faithful receive him. In other words, the *presence* of Christ in the sacrament does not depend upon the faith of the worshippers, but on the faithfulness of Christ. On the other hand, the *reception* of Christ by the communicant does depend upon the faith of the communicant, and (in the Pauline sense) on his worthiness (1 Cor. 11.27-29). Eucharistic reality is in the hands of God: only the apprehension of that reality depends upon the human element. If we believe that Christ is present invisibly in his spiritual body, among the members of his mystical body, there is no inherent difficulty in the belief that he truly gives himself to us through his sacramental body received in communion by faith with thanksgiving.

In controversial writings, sacramental grace is sometimes made to appear as a kind of 'impersonal fluid'. Again, Protestant thinkers are entirely right in rejecting such a conception. Sacramental grace is essentially and really a *personal* influence, mediated through covenanted means. Christ is personally present to faith in the sacrament; and so imparts himself personally to those who apprehend his presence. The faithful, by *their* presence in *his* presence, cannot fail to come under his influence. That influence is the 'reward' of obedience to the command, 'Do this in remembrance of me.' It is imparted at the deepest personal level, according to Christ's own ordinance, by the faithful reception of the sacramental species in communion. As Article 28 (of the Thirty-nine Articles) insists, 'the Body of Christ is given, taken, and eaten, in the Supper, only after an heavenly and spiritual manner. And the mean whereby the Body of Christ is received and eaten in the Supper is Faith.' Faith is essentially a personal response to a personal, spiritual, presence. The approach of the communicant to the Risen Lord in the sacrament is an intensely personal encounter. It can never be adequately expressed in impersonal semi-mechanical terms.

Although therefore we must hold firmly to the doctrine of the real presence of Christ in the sacramental species, there is a very real danger in over-defining the manner of his presence. For instance, the doctrine of transubstantiation is an attempt to define the manner of the Lord's presence in the consecrated species in terms of the medieval philosophy of substance and accidents. Without doubt, it is a help to those who are prepared to think in this way. Experience has shown, however, that it can be a definite barrier to real understanding for those who naturally think in other categories. Provided that we safeguard the *fact* of Christ's presence, spiritually, mystically, and sacramentally, in the Eucharist; and provided we approach him in so great a sacrament with faith and in worship; there does not appear to be any need to define the manner of his sacramental presence with greater precision. Sufficient is it that by his presence we should be lifted up into the heavenly places, to share in the worship offered eternally before the throne of God and to be fed with the Bread of Life.

What then is consecration? What is 'effected' by the great eucharistic prayer? Except in the face of impersonal and somewhat mechanical conceptions, which are wholly out of place in the discussion of the Eucharist, such questions could hardly arise. Indeed there is little evidence that consecration presented any problem whatever to the Church in the age of the Fathers. In the Eucharist the whole of human life was brought to God, and consecrated by him; the Church had the experience of being the Body of Christ, united mystically to its Lord; and the experience of receiving, and feeding upon, the Body of Christ. The practice of the Christian religion was supremely a life of personal discipleship to a Lord known and loved; in an alien and often antagonistic world. Vastly different was the situation in medieval times. The layman then was often only nominally Christian. The ministry was entirely professionalized. The doctrine of the Real Presence was largely divorced from the experience of regular and frequent communion. It is small wonder that the idea grew up that the priest had *in himself* the *power* to 'make Christ's body'. Mechanical views of grace were the order of the day, and a mechanical theory of consecration was the obvious corollary. To-day the Church is recovering a more primitive and more eirenic view of the act of consecration. The celebrant in the Eucharist is the mouthpiece of the Church as it is assembled for worship. What he does he does only in the name of the Church, and in the context of the worship of the whole Church, in heaven and on earth. The worship of the Church is its Thanksgiving (*eucharistia*) for all the mighty works of God, and in particular for the salvation offered to the world in our Lord Jesus Christ. The bread and the wine are consecrated, they become holy, by the Church's thanksgiving to God over them. This is the ancient view, in line entirely with the Jewish conception of the blessing of bread and cup. There is no need to attempt any further 'explanation'. In recovering this primitive view, the Church can surely recover its peace and unity in Christ.

THE DOCTRINE OF SACRIFICE

The need for sacrifice as a means of approach to God is deeply ingrained not only in the generality of ancient religions, but supremely in the Old Testament. In the scriptures of Israel sacrifice is conceived not primarily in the sense of propitiating an angry God, though this overtone is not entirely absent. Rather is it the appointed means of expressing the honour and worship due from man to God Almighty. It is laid down expressly in the most ancient code of the law, and repeated in the deuteronomic legislation, that 'none shall appear before me empty' (Exod. 34.20; Deut. 16.16). The offering of something costly, with which the worshipper can identify himself, is the one and only way of access to the divine presence.

The fulminations of the Old Testament prophets were not directed against the sacrificial system as such, but against an empty ritual observance unaccompanied by a moral life. The most frequently quoted text, 'I desired mercy, and not sacrifice; and the knowledge of God more than burnt offerings' (Hos. 6.6), is a statement of priorities rather than an outright condemnation of sacrifice. 'Mercy' is the human analogue of the 'loving-kindness' of God: to 'know' God is primarily to obey him. The 'outward and visible sign' of obedience without the 'thing signified' is valueless. This is not to say that true human obedience and worship are not to be expressed through the offering of sacrifice. Our Lord's attitude to the ancient law leaves no room for the view that the outward observance is necessarily without value. But he too insists on a right order of priorities when he comments, 'these ought ye to have done, and not to leave the other undone' (Mt. 23.23).

We have seen already that the writers of the New Testament found the language of sacrifice an essential vehicle for the description of Christ's work of redemption. Such language is used not only by the apostles John and Paul, and by the author of Hebrews, but by our Lord himself (Mark 10.45). We cannot suppose this well-nigh universal reliance on the language of sacrifice to be a

kind of hang-over from primitive religion, and therefore
ultimately mistaken. It speaks to us of something deep
down in the nature of things: the sacrificial self-giving
of God Incarnate. The New Testament also uses a modi-
fied language of sacrifice in speaking of the Eucharist.
We have seen too that this is something more than a
fruitful line of thought. It is the means of access to the
deepest mystery of the eucharistic worship of the Church,
which is a participation here and now in the eternal
worship of heaven.

Medieval religion, however, was not content with the
restrained biblical insight into the sacrificial aspect of
the Eucharist. Instead, it elaborated a doctrine according
to which Christ suffers afresh in each celebration of the
Mass. Though these views were not endorsed apparently
by the greatest of medieval theologians, they were nevertheless widespread, and formed the basis not only of popular teaching but also of the enormous vogue of masses for
the dead. The sacrifice on Calvary was supposed to avail
for original sin, and the sacrifice of the Mass for actual
sins. Hence the multiplication of solitary masses, and the
endowment of chantries. These developments, completely
out of touch with the religion of the New Testament, had
the effect of reducing Christianity to the status of an
actuarial system. The reformers very rightly were in
revolt against this popular 'theology', and the whole
system of religion to which it led and by which it was
fortified. Article 31 is a clear expression of the reformation attitude to the old religion; and condemns the
'sacrifices of Masses' in language which is a trifle strong,
but in the circumstances by no means unfair. The careful wording of the article as a whole does not however
deny the sacrificial character of the Eucharist in any

particular; though it may truly be said that the reformed English Rite of the Book of Common Prayer does less than justice to this aspect of eucharistic worship. Nor does the article deny the appropriateness of the commemoration of the faithful departed within the context of the Eucharist; though again that commemoration is contained within very narrow limits in the prayer for the whole state of Christ's Church. We may readily admit that the temper of the times required that the main emphasis of the eucharistic teaching of the reformers be placed elsewhere: they lived in an age when the laity had become for all practical purposes non-communicant.

All this chapter of errors seems to derive fundamentally from the general prevalence of an unbiblical view of the character of sacrifice: a misunderstanding in which the reformers shared, hardly less than the medieval Church. The Bible nowhere takes the view that God requires the suffering and death of a sacrificial victim. Such a view is wholly alien to the Biblical revelation of the character of God. Even in the sacrificial system of the Old Testament the death of the victim is incidental to the offering of the *life* to Almighty God. Still more in the Epistle to the Hebrews is it clear that sacrifice in the true sense consists in the willing offering of the one perfect Life. Christ's sufferings and death are not in themselves the sacrifice to which the Christian Church looks for its redemption. His death was the work of evil men, the logical outcome of man's rebellion against God. The sacrifice to which the Church looks for its redemption is the entering of the Risen and Ascended Christ into the heavenly places: there to present himself, and mankind in him, before the Father. We are redeemed by the interceding presence of the Ascended

Christ in heaven, rather than strictly *only* by the death on
Calvary. This essentially Biblical truth the reformers
largely failed to see: it had been totally overlaid by
mechanical and feudal views of the Atonement for hun-
dreds of years. Hence the absence from the English Rite
of the specific thanksgiving for the Lord's 'mighty
Resurrection and glorious Ascension' which had characterized the liturgy of the primitive Church. With the
recovery of the Biblical view of sacrifice the way opens
for a return to primitive wholeness and a recovery of
unity between Christians of separated traditions.

The Eucharist is sacrificial in the sense that, like the
Ascension itself, it brings the perfect manhood of Christ,
and ourselves in him, before the Throne of grace. Moreover, one purpose of the Old Testament sacrifices, perhaps
the most significant, humanly speaking, was communion
with God. The Eucharist also, as the Christian offering
of praise and thanksgiving to God in Christ, is completed
in the act of communion. 'We have an altar, whereof
they have no right to eat which serve the tabernacle. . . .
Jesus also, that he might sanctify the people with his
own blood, suffered without the gate. Let us go forth
therefore unto him. . . . By him therefore let us offer
the sacrifice of praise to God continually. . . . But to do
good and to communicate forget not: for with such
sacrifices God is well pleased.' (Heb. 13.10-16)

Very properly the English Rite, in its prayer of consecration, insists that the sacrifice of Christ is the only
sacrifice which avails for sin. In phrases of which only a
single word (satisfaction) betrays the unbiblical view
of sacrifice inherited from the medieval Church, the
sacrifice of Christ is described as 'a full, perfect, and
sufficient sacrifice, oblation, and satisfaction, for the sins

of the whole world'. The Eucharist neither repeats, nor adds to, the one sacrifice of Christ. It is rather a bringing of that one all-sufficient sacrifice before the Father; so that the Church is identified in the Spirit with Christ, and itself is offered in him. In this sense of the word, which is faithful to the thought of the New Testament, the Eucharist is a sacrificial act; and in this sense it is legitimate to speak of the 'sacrifice of the Mass'.

Thus we see that it is theologically impossible to celebrate the Eucharist, by whatever name we may denote the service, without offering the 'sacrifice of the Mass' in the New Testament sense of the word 'sacrifice'. The sacrifice of the Mass is one aspect, and not the least important aspect, of what every single celebration of the Eucharist effects. The most protestant-minded low Churchman, just as much as the most ardent Romanist, offers the sacrifice of the Mass, in the true sense of those much misused words, every time he celebrates the Holy Communion. Simply by his obedience to the Lord's command, 'Do this in remembrance of me', he brings the Lord's perfect sacrifice before the Father. Thereby Christ is offered: and the Church in him. Sacrifice, in the New Testament sense, is an essential aspect of the total eucharistic act.

CHURCH ORDER

'Let all things be done decently and in order,' wrote St. Paul (1 Cor. 14.40). No group of organized Christians is likely to dissent from his dictum: but not all groups understand it in the same way.

The problem of Church Order and its bearing upon the Eucharist is something essentially modern. Splinter-groups, rival bishops in the same diocese, even rival

Popes, have their place in Christian history. But until the Reformation the territorial division of the Church Catholic into dioceses, each governed by the bishop and served by the ancient three-fold ministry, was taken for granted. While there is considerable uncertainty as to how the Catholic system of Church Order arose in the immediately post-apostolic period, there is no evidence whatever of any rival system for fifteen centuries. The Eucharist of the one Church was therefore that celebrated either by the local bishop, or in communion with him.

The division of the Church resulting from the Reformation differs from all previous schisms in that it perpetuates widely diverse systems of Church Order; which in themselves constitute a more formidable barrier to unity than do the differences of doctrine or emphasis within the fold of any single ecclesiastical system. The real tragedy of Christendom lies precisely in the fact that division has broken the visible fellowship of Christians around the one table of the Lord. On the other hand, the existence of the Anglican Communion is a standing proof that unity around the one table is still a possibility in spite of wide differences of eucharistic doctrine. But the denominational barriers have succeeded in dividing the Church into separate water-tight compartments, overlapping territorially but sharing no visible fellowship around the table of the Lord.

When we inquire what is the root cause of the modern state of schism, we find it to lie in a fundamental difference of view of the nature of authority. In those churches which have retained the ancient Catholic order (Orthodox, Roman, and Anglican), authority is conceived as devolving from above: from Christ, through the apostles, to the episcopate. In the Roman communion, it is true, the Pope exercises an authority, as Vicar of Christ and Successor of Peter, superior to that exercised by the rest of the episcopate; but the general pattern of an authority devolving from above is otherwise similar to that recognized in the Orthodox and Anglican communions. Every minister, and every layman, is 'a man under authority'. In the various Protestant bodies, however, an entirely different view of authority prevails. It goes without saying, of course, that the authority of Christ is recognized as paramount: but that authority is not conceived as being mediated to the Church through an historically-continuous succession of ministers. The use of such phrases as 'the priesthood of all believers', or 'the parity of ministers', seems to point to a concept of authority as something which is exercised democratically. There is, of course, a sense in which Christ speaks to his Church through the common mind of its members, reached through the guidance of the Spirit, and discovered in processes which are democratic in appearance. Such processes have their place in the Catholic system of Church Order. But in contrasting the two systems, it seems hardly unfair to say that in Protestantism authority is conceived as from below. No English free-church minister would dream of describing himself as 'a man under authority'. A Catholic priest would not dream of questioning such a description of himself. In this simple fact lies the essential difference between the two systems of Church Order.

This is not the place to enter into a full discussion of Church Order, and the reunion of Christendom. In the interest of mutual understanding, however, particularly as regards the celebration of the Eucharist, certain remarks may legitimately be made with regard to the episcopal office.

The Churches which maintain the ancient Catholic order, weakened though they are by schism, find in the office of the bishop a real focus of unity. The bishop is more than a merely external fount of authority. He is intended to be, and undoubtedly is, a Father-in-God to his people, and a minister to the lower orders of the ministry. The authority which he exercises is a fatherly authority. The service which he renders to his flock is the service of a shepherd. As father and shepherd he draws into unity the family and flock committed by Christ to his care. When the bishop presides at the Eucharist in his own Cathedral Church, or in any other Church in his diocese, in a unique sense he is the earthly representative of the Lord who presided at the Supper on the night in which he was betrayed. And every parish priest, presiding at the Eucharist in his own parish, does so as the deputy of the bishop from whom he receives his cure. In this way the sense of the visible unity of the Church, and the necessity for that unity, are kept clearly in mind. Unity is essentially something *given* by Christ to his Church. It is emphatically not something which *we* engineer. It is from above, not from below. If unity is to be had at all, it must be accepted in humility from the giver, on his terms; in the same way as salvation itself. To us who experience Catholic order from the inside, the office of the bishop safeguards this fundamental truth.

But truth must never be held in a spirit of arrogance. Other groups of Christians, deprived by history of any direct inside experience of Catholic order, have obvious and intelligible difficulty in understanding the unique value and function of the episcopal office. Only by patience and humility, restraint and charity, can a sense of the bishop's function as a focus of unity be conveyed across denominational barriers. The Churches which have inherited the Catholic tradition must continue to hold it as a priceless possession, to be shared ultimately by all, when the Spirit has prepared the way for the restoration of that visible unity which was given by Christ to his Church.

8

One Bread, One Body

The previous chapter posed a question, by its title: drawn of course from St. Paul's first epistle to the clique-ridden Church of Corinth. The question was not, however, answered in so many words. Instead we dwelt on the unity of the Church and the divisions of Christians. That the divisions of Christians have broken the *visible* unity of the Church cannot be denied. But in the hopeful ecumenical atmosphere of to-day we dare not say that unity in every sense is shattered. This chapter, by its title, drawn from the same epistle, makes an assertion. Even in the ecumenical situation of to-day, this assertion is none the less challenging. Can we justify it?

I must begin where I am myself, a member of the world-wide Anglican Communion. Within that communion wide differences of eucharistic theology and practice prevail: only a little less wide than those which separate Rome and Geneva. Yet visible unity exists also; and miraculously the Anglican Communion holds together by the grace of God. Now it is not the slightest use suggesting that this visible unity does not involve tension. For some of us the tension is almost unbearable; and from time to time is the cause of a certain lack of charity, at any rate between the extreme wings. The Old

Adam is still very much alive in a good many of us, lamentable though this may be. And lack of charity is easily disguised as sound theology.

An Anglo-Catholic attending a celebration of the Holy Communion according to the extreme Evangelical tradition can be distinctly uncomfortable. So many of the familiar landmarks are missing. The words of the liturgy are, shall we say, the familiar words of the Prayer Book of 1662; but there is a 'bareness' and an 'atmosphere' which he feels to be something of a barrier to true unity, and somewhat difficult to penetrate. Yet our visiting Anglo-Catholic receives the true sacrament of the Body and Blood of the Lord; and if his heart is in the right place he overcomes his uneasiness, and knows that he has fellowship in Christ with a sincere group of Christ's disciples. An Evangelical, on the other hand, attending the Eucharist in an Anglo-Catholic parish, may be equally uncomfortable, though for the opposite reason. He deplores the use of vestments, incense, and ceremonial: and may even question the right of an Anglican clergyman to interpret the Prayer Book in such a way. Yet again, our visitor receives the Lord in communion by faith with thanksgiving; and if his heart is in the right place he knows that he has fellowship in Christ with a sincere group of fellow-Anglicans, in spite of the genuflexions and crossings which go on all around him. Here are the tensions of the visible unity which is ours by the grace of God. Here too is the meaning of visible unity in the midst of theological division.

What is the real basis of unity in such a case as this? It is certainly not the existence of a common mind on such matters as the Real Presence and the Eucharistic Sacrifice: on these matters there is division. The basis of

H

unity is devotion to the one Lord within a fellowship which is historically given. If each has fellowship with Christ, each has fellowship with his fellow Christians. The true unity which Christ gives, even to one part of his Church, transcends our individual differences, and holds us together by grace. We meet at the one table of the Lord, and in him we are brothers. Perhaps the tensions are only those to be expected between brothers in a sinful world, where truth is often misunderstood and charity strained. But brothers we are in Christ.

So much for the situation within Anglicanism, which is relatively simple. Can we now extend this concept of unity at the deep level, in the face of our present divisions of doctrine and practice, so as to bridge the denominational barriers? The important point to remember is that fellowship between Christians is not based primarily on exact theological agreement, valuable and desirable as this may be, but on fellowship with Christ. Fallen human nature tends always towards division. Unity and fellowship are supernatural gifts—from Christ to his Church. Fundamentally, unity is the bond by which each faithful Christian is held to his Lord. It is only through the hidden life of the mystical body of Christ that I find unity with any fellow-Christian whatever. Because we feed on the same Lord, draw our life from the same Christ; *therefore*, there is unity between us at the deep level: and for no other reason.

Clearly, unity in this deep sense transcends denominational barriers. We ask then, what are these denominational barriers? They are simply the limits up to which our forefathers in the faith were prepared to recognize their unity in Christ: the limits beyond which they were not prepared to concede fellowship. We have inherited the barriers. We cannot simply over-ride them; behaving as though they do not exist, communicating indiscriminately at one another's altars, and claiming for ourselves exceptional breadth of mind and Christian charity. Our loyalty to Christ is a loyalty given and known within a particular tradition, or ecclesiastical system. To be faithful to Christ *is* to be faithful to that part of his mystical body in which we are nurtured. But we must apply St. Paul's words of warning to separated communions as well as to individual Christians. 'The eye cannot say unto the hand, I have no need of thee: nor again the head to the feet, I have no need of you' (1 Cor. 12.21). In other words, a real unity exists within the mystical body in spite of our denominational barriers: a unity given by Christ, but formally denied by our ecclesiastical alignments. In this situation, faithfulness to Christ demands not only loyalty to that part of the mystical body in which we are nurtured, but also recognition of the real membership of communions other than our own in that mystical body. This surely is the driving force of the Ecumenical Movement, which is the great new fact of twentieth-century Christianity.

Once we learn to look at the situation ecumenically, the denominational barriers begin to lose their significance. Unity at the deep level can and does exist in Christ between separated traditions, and between individuals on opposite sides of an ecclesiastical boundary. By what criterion are we to discern bodies of Christians with whom true unity at the deep level already exists in Christ? Are we to include this group? Must we exclude that? Where are we to draw the boundaries? Are we in the Anglican Communion entitled to mark out a

boundary on the basis of the possession of Catholic order
and the historic episcopate? The familiar 'branch theory'
is the attempt to do so. Are certain other communions
entitled to mark out a boundary on the basis of the common possession of a 'reformed' theology, so excluding
both Roman and Eastern Christianity?

The answer is that it is not for *us* to mark out boundaries at all. Nor is it for us to attempt to disregard some
of the boundaries inherited from the past, while inking
in others even more boldly. The left arm and the right
arm may well be doing different work, but they are still
parts of the same body. Only Christ can know who serves
him faithfully. Only he can know the limits of his own
mystical body. Only he can know to what groups of men,
professing some form of the Christian faith, he grants
a real share in the hidden life of his mystical body. Even
though, by historical accident and human perversity,
some may have lost what we Anglicans believe to be of
the *esse* of the Church, yet only Christ can give or
withhold a share in the life of his Kingdom. It is not for
us to mark out boundaries, even on the basis of what we
believe to be the true theology of the Christian Church.
On the contrary we must by all means recognize the
unity which all faithful Christians have in Christ as partakers of the one bread. Unity at the deepest level is a
supernatural gift. All that we can do is to recognize it in
thankfulness.

Are we then to be completely 'fuzzy', disregarding
the theological issues which still divide Christendom,
treating our differences of order or doctrine as matters
of no ultimate significance? By no means. To do so would
be to trifle with the most holy things of our Christian
experience, to be faithless to the truth in Christ as we

have received it from the past. It is entirely right that Anglicans should seek to enter into relations of full communion with other separated churches (horrible plural), only on the basis of the acceptance of a common episcopal order. It is entirely right that Roman Catholics should seek to draw all Christian men into visible communion with the Holy See: entirely right that the various Protestant bodies should seek a wider unity on the basis of a 'reformed' theology. Why? Because in each case the insight in question is fundamental to the true nature of the Church *as each group understands it*. We must be faithful to the truth as we see it. Yet at the same time we must be inclusive in our sympathies; and we must have the humility to recognize that the truth is a bigger thing than our own apprehension of it. In ways we do not yet understand, the several emphases of this divided Christendom (even where they diverge most sharply) may be complementary aspects of the one truth as it is in Christ. We must pray that the Lord of truth will lead us to acknowledge the fulness of truth: and so lead us into the visible unity which is agreeable to his will.

We began this brief study of the central act of Christian worship by asserting that every Eucharist that the Church celebrates is linked in space, in time, and in eternity with every other. By now the meaning of that assertion should have become clear, and its implications apparent. 'Do this in remembrance of me.' The Church has obeyed; and even in its divided state its several parts still obey. Thereby the chain of continuous worship is forged, which links the Eucharist of the divided Church of to-day back to the Eucharist of the one undivided Church of ancient times, and to the Supper of the Lord. 'As often as ye eat this bread, and drink this cup, ye do shew the Lord's death till he come.' Even in our tragic division we still look forward to the coming of the one Lord at the end of time, to call his one Church to the Marriage Supper of the Lamb. Anticipating here and now that final consummation, we share already, though transiently and imperfectly, in union and fellowship with our Redeemer. We are in him, and he in us, through our sharing here and now in 'the bread which we break'. Thereby the link in space between one altar and another altar on earth is forged. Distance is annihilated; and we have communion in Christ with the next parish, with the next diocese, with the 'churches' of our own communion at the antipodes. What are we to say about the link in space with the 'church' down the street, living its own life of fellowship, separated from ourselves by a denominational barrier? In Christ that link exists already. How long shall we be content to deny it?

Do we really want visible unity here on earth? Are we content to meet our Risen Lord, as we do to-day, around separated tables? Is the Church of God a restaurant, or a Father's home? Do we long for the time when these historic divisions will have become utterly meaningless, and schism will have ceased? These are the ultimate questions for our separated communions to-day.

The Spirit has led us to recognize our deep unity in Christ. He has led us to the point where we are not content to remain as we are, united at the deep level but separated outwardly in organization, doctrine, and practice. The change in atmosphere in the past half-century has been enormous. This is entirely the work of the Spirit among us: and the Ecumenical Movement is the outward manifestation of the inner change of heart. If the 'churches' continue to follow faithfully the guidance of the Spirit we shall be led on to the point where outward and visible unity is achieved. The obstacles, both of theology and of order, still look well-nigh insuperable. But we know the declared will of God. The Lord prayed that his Church might be one; 'that they all may be one; as thou, Father, art in me, and I in thee, that they also may be one in us: that the world may believe that thou hast sent me' (John 17.21). We have faith that, in spite of the apparently insuperable obstacles, the Lord's prayer for unity must be answered. It will, of course, be answered in eternity. We believe that it will be answered in this world of time.

But how? Perhaps the Church of South India is a pointer. Perhaps the reunion schemes of North India and Ceylon are pointers. The time will surely come when we shall accept validation of our separated ministries from one another, either reciprocally or unilaterally, in Christian humility. Or perhaps we may be led to visible unity in some other quite unexpected way, which is beyond our present understanding. Of one thing we can be sure: The Spirit will lead us back to visible unity if only we follow his guidance; because this is manifestly the will of the Lord, and the condition of our accomplishing our share in his work on earth. 'O the depth of the riches both of the wisdom and knowledge of God! how unsearchable are his judgements, and his ways past finding out!' (Rom. 11.33) In this faith we follow, humbly waiting till we are shown the way, God's way, to visible unity.

Christ is not divided. We are 'one bread, one body', in him, in spite of the outward divisions of theology, organization and practice. May we not then see something prophetic in the ancient prayer? 'As this bread that is broken was scattered upon the mountains, and gathered together, and became one, so let thy Church be gathered together from the ends of the earth into thy kingdom: for thine is the glory and the power through Jesus Christ for ever.' (Didache 9.4)

Index

Index